DISCOVERING POETRY

BY ELIZABETH DREW

DISCOVERING POETRY

POETRY:
A Modern Guide

THE NOVEL:
A Modern Guide to Fifteen English Masterpieces

THE LITERATURE OF GOSSIP:
Nine English Letterwriters

DISCOVERING POETRY

BY *Elizabeth Drew*

W · W · NORTON & COMPANY · INC ·

NEW YORK

W. W. Norton & Company, Inc. is also the publisher of *The Norton Anthology of English Literature*, edited by M. H. Abrams, Robert M. Adams, David Daiches, E. Talbot Donaldson, George H. Ford, Samuel Holt Monk, and Hallett Smith; *The American Tradition in Literature*, edited by Sculley Bradley, Richmond Croom Beatty, and E. Hudson Long; *World Masterpieces*, edited by Maynard Mack, Kenneth Douglas, Howard E. Hugo, Bernard M. W. Knox, John C. McGalliard, P. M. Pasinetti, and René Wellek; *The Norton Reader*, edited by Arthur M. Eastman, Caesar R. Blake, Hubert M. English, Jr., Alan B. Howes, Robert T. Lenaghan, Leo F. McNamara, and James Rosier; and the NORTON CRITICAL EDITIONS, in hardcover and paperbound: authoritative texts, together with the leading critical interpretations, of major works of British, American, and Continental literature.

To Joan and George
With Affectionate Gratitude

I was nearly a fortnight at Mr. John Snook's and a few days at old Mr. Dilke's. Nothing worth speaking of happened at either place. I took down some thin paper and wrote on it a little poem call'd St. Agnes' Eve.

JOHN KEATS. LETTER TO GEORGE KEATS, FEBRUARY 24, 1819.

PREFACE

> Of *genius, in the fine arts, the only infallible sign is the widening the sphere of human sensibility, for the delight, honour, and benefit of human nature. Genius is the introduction of a new element into the intellectual universe: or, if that be not allowed, it is the application of powers to objects on which they had not before been exercised, or the employment of them in such a manner as to produce effects hitherto unknown. What is all this but an advance, or a conquest, made by the soul of the poet? Is it to be supposed that the reader can make progress of this kind, like an Indian prince or general—stretched on his palanquin, and borne by his slaves? No; he is invigorated and inspirited by his leader, in order that he may exert himself; for he cannot proceed in quiescence, he cannot be carried like a dead weight. Therefore, to create taste is to call forth and bestow power....*

> [WILLIAM WORDSWORTH. Essay Supplementary to Preface. 1815.]

THE whole of this book is really an expansion of the passage quoted here. It is an effort to try and discover in what poetic genius consists, and in what ways we may best train ourselves to recognize and to enjoy it.

But in any such enquiry, we are immediately challenged at the outset by a pertinent and disquieting ques-

tion. Why write *about* poetry, when the poets themselves
are there to speak? Everything they have to say, they
can very well say for themselves: do we not 'murder
to dissect'? For there is much truth in what Sir Walter
Raleigh said when he set out to lecture about Christina
Rossetti. 'The worst of it is you cannot lecture on really
pure poetry any more than you can talk about the in-
gredients of really pure water—it is adulterated, meth-
ylated, sanded poetry that makes the best lectures. The
only thing that Christina makes me want to do, is cry,
not lecture.' And it is true that when we criticize poetry,
when we analyze form and rhythm and metre and im-
agery and words, and as much of the whole technical
mystery of transforming experiences into language as
we can, at the end we are sometimes reminded of the
comment of Mutt to Jeff on hearing that water was two
parts hydrogen to one part oxygen: 'Good heavens, ain't
there no *water* in it?'

It is obvious from the number of people who do read
poetry, and who do not read criticism, that there is no
need whatever to read books about poetry in order to
appreciate it. And indeed it cannot be over-emphasized
that it is the direct experience of poetry itself, the ap-
prehension of the poetic vision and the poetic world and
the poetic act, which is what communicates that 'power'
of which Wordsworth speaks. It is only the reading of
poetry which can teach the love of poetry, it is only the
direct contact with the stuff itself. That is why I have
filled this book with poetry—poetry of all ages and
kinds and colours—and am never away from it for long.
I repeat, it is only the reading of poetry which can bring
the love of it, and it is quite possible to have a genuine

taste for poetry with very little discrimination about it. It is, moreover, much better to have a real delight in the reading of even poor poetry than to have an arid intellectual knowledge of critical theory. But to have both enthusiasm *and* discrimination is surely the best of all.

To have both enthusiasm and discrimination about poetry involves having two different kinds of experience about it, for the pleasures of criticism are different from the pleasures of poetry, though they are inter-related. Reading poetry as it should be read is an act of apprehension: criticism is the analysis by an intellectual process of that apprehension. It is an act of comprehension. Criticism cannot communicate the 'power'. What it can do is to develop faculty. Everyone can read poetry, and yet, as Bacon said, 'Naturall Abilities are like Naturall Plants, they need Proyning by Study': or as Wordsworth again declares, 'an accurate taste in poetry is an acquired talent.' For the art of reading poetry is to find what is there; and that is not as simple as it sounds. It implies that when we have felt delight in a poem, we should be capable of analyzing that delight. That we should start asking ourselves questions. What is it which makes certain arrangements of words have an effect upon us unlike anything else? What is that effect? Wherein does one poem differ from another in effect? Why is one better than another? What is the value of poetry? What are the secrets of its technique? Above all, what is the relation of poetry to life? Criticism really springs from curiosity. Sooner or later the curious reader inevitably finds himself asking these questions, and from that moment he is a critic. Inevitably, too, he will henceforward find that the alertness of reading which his new curiosity has engendered makes him more keenly sensitive and responsive to the power of poetry, and more apt to receive it and to receive more of it. This is what makes criticism of real help and of real value in the discovery of poetry. A knowledge of and an interest in geography, surveying, architecture, history and sociology is not the same thing as a love of travel, and the glamour and glory of foreign lands and cities can be apprehended without the help of any of them. Yet we would sooner have a guide who could deepen and enrich our experience of the unknown by the addition of such knowledge. And the same thing is true of travel in 'the realms of gold'.

CONTENTS

ACKNOWLEDGMENTS

For permission to use selections the author is indebted to the following:

Robert O. Ballou, Publisher, for D. H. Lawrence's *Piano*

Jonathan Cape, Ltd., for W. H. Davies' *Sweet Chance*

Chatto & Windus for T. H. White's *And on what beautiful morning*

E. P. Dutton & Company, Inc., for Samuel Butler's *Not on sad Stygian shore*

Faber & Faber, Ltd., for T. S. Eliot's *A Cooking Egg, The Waste Land*

The Hogarth Press for C. Day Lewis' *The Magnetic Mountain*; Richard Eberhart's *Request for Offering*

Henry Holt & Company for Walter de la Mare's *The Song of the Mad Prince*; Edward Thomas' *Cockcrow*

Little, Brown & Company for Emily Dickinson's *I got so I could hear his name*

Horace Liveright, Inc., for E. E. Cummings' *Among these red pieces of day*

The Macmillan Company for William Butler Yeats' *The Folly of Being Comforted*; Thomas Hardy's *Neutral Tones, I say I'll seek her*

The Oxford University Press for Robert Bridges' *On a Dead Child*; Gerard Manley Hopkins' *Carrion Comfort, Margaret, The Windhover*

Charles Scribner's Sons for Francis Thompson's *In No Strange Land*; Alice Meynell's *The Two Poets*

DISCOVERING

POETRY

POETRY AND THE POET

I.

WHAT is poetry? Let us listen to some.

Wake: the silver dusk returning
Up the beach of darkness brims
And the ship of sunrise burning
Strands upon the eastern rims.

*

Bring me my Bow of burning gold!
Bring me my Arrows of desire!
Bring me my Spear! O clouds, unfold!
Bring me my Chariot of fire!

*

Her feet beneath her petticoat
Like little mice stole in and out
As if they feared the light;
But O! she dances such a way
No sun upon an Easter day
Is half so fine a sight.

*

So when or you or I are made
A fable, song, or fleeting shade;
All love, all liking, all delight
Lies drown'd with us in endless night.

*

I got so I could hear his name
Without—
Tremendous gain!—
That stop-sensation in my Soul
And thunder in the room.

All these are poetry, and from them we should be able to find some answer to that direct challenge which meets us at once on the outset of our quest. What *is* poetry?

There are almost as many definitions of poetry as there are poets and critics who have written about it. The trouble with most of them is that they tend to be so abstract and nebulous. 'Poetry is a spirit ... it comes we know not whence.' 'Poetry is an intuition into the hidden nature of things.' 'Poetry is the breath and finer spirit of all knowledge.' 'Poetry is that which comprehends all science, and that to which all science must be referred.' 'Poetry is a continuous substance or energy.' 'Poetry is a glimpse of the divine.' But whatever poetry is, it is not something else. It is not religion, or philosophy, or aesthetics, or science, or knowledge. It is poetry. And poetry, as 'Q' said, is the stuff poets have written. This again, however, is the snake swallowing its own tail; it does not get us very much further. It again only reminds us that poetry is something unlike anything else, and something difficult to define. It is in the same class of definition as Emily Dickinson's—'If I read a book ... and I feel physically as if the top of my head were taken off, I know that is poetry ... is there any other way?'

Ultimately, perhaps, there *is* no other way of knowing. That is, poetry is a particular stimulus, which provides a certain kind of response in the right sort of reader. And the whole business of criticism is an effort to try and discover what the nature of that stimulus is, and what the nature of that response is and what makes the right sort of reader.

Abstractions do not help us: they cannot supply the answer to that immediate and practical question: what is the difference between

> Wake: the silver dusk returning
> Up the beach of darkness brims

and 'Wake, the sun is rising'? Or between

> So when you or I are made
> A fable, song or fleeting shade;
> All love, all liking, all delight
> Lies drown'd with us in endless night.

and 'When we die, our love will end'?

The verses and the bare statements have the same meaning; they are different ways of conveying the same sense or thought or idea. That is clear; and it is equally clear that that is all they do have in common. Beyond that, at once we feel that in the poetry we are in a different world from that of the prose statements. It is different in two ways. First, *its mode of experiencing the thought or idea or subject or material presented to it, is different*; and secondly, *the words in which the experience is communicated are different*. In those two facts lie the whole theory and practice of poetry.

The raw material of poetry is human experience: all poetry is made from that. Not only from rare and subtle and mysterious and spiritual and abstract and esoteric experiences, but from all and every form of human experience. As Wordsworth says: 'it is the honorable characteristic of poetry that its materials are to be found in every subject which can interest the human mind.' Poetry is made from birth and death, from childhood, youth, and old age; from love, jealousy, ambition, faith, cruelty, kindliness, rage, loyalty, laughter; from the solid commonplaces on which all living is based, and the most subtle and recondite mood and movement of the individual personality; from the ecstasy of the mystic and the rape of the lock; from the fall of man, and an idiot boy; from a rainbow and a rabbit; from *la belle dame sans merci* and the servant girl coming downstairs in the morning.

But the poet apprehends and interprets this general experience in ways which belong to him alone.

2.

ON a certain October day in the year 1816, Charles Cowden Clarke told his young friend John Keats that he had been lent a copy of Chapman's translation of Homer, and he asked Keats to come and explore it with him that evening. Keats went, and the two friends read on through the night till dawn, not beginning at the beginning and working through the epics, but picking out what Cowden Clarke calls 'the famousest passages', or 'looking into' it, as Keats himself expressed it. Then the young medical student walked back to his own home in another part of London as the day was breaking. When Cowden Clarke came down to a late breakfast next morning at 10 o'clock he found on the table an envelope in Keats's handwriting. Inside was a sheet of paper containing a sonnet:

> Much have I travell'd in the realms of gold,
> And many goodly states and kingdoms seen;
> Round many western islands have I been
> Which bards in fealty to Apollo hold.
> Oft of one wide expanse had I been told
> That deep-brow'd Homer ruled as his demesne:
> Yet never could I judge what men might mean
> Till I heard Chapman speak out loud and bold:
> Then felt I like some watcher of the skies

When a new planet swims into his ken;
Or like stout Cortez, when with wond'ring eyes
He stared at the Pacific—and all his men
Look'd at each other with a wild surmise—
Silent, upon a peak in Darien.

These two young men had had a common experience
the night before. They had read a book together. Cow-
den Clarke has left a description of that evening in
prose. Keats has left a poem. We should surely be able
to discover something of what is vital to the nature of
poetry and the poet by a contrast of the two methods
of communication and an examination of the particular
character of each.

3.

THEY have one great point of similarity. With both, the
experience has become *words*. It is no longer the actual
reading of a book which Charles Cowden Clarke shared
with John Keats. Both the prose and the poetry are col-
lections of words, and everything which we as readers
receive from reading them, reaches us through the words
the writers have chosen.

Cowden Clarke tells us the facts of the matter as
they appeared to him.

'A beautiful copy of the folio edition of Chapman's
translation of Homer had been lent me. It was the prop-
erty of Mr. Alsager, the gentleman who for years had
contributed no small share of celebrity to the great repu-
tation of the *Times* newspaper by the masterly manner
in which he conducted the money-market department
of that journal. . . .

'Well, then, we were put in possession of the Homer
of Chapman, and to work we went, turning to some of
the "famousest" passages, as we had scrappily known
them in Pope's version. . . .'

Then follows an account of some of the passages, and of the arrival of the sonnet next morning.

Now let us read the sonnet again and see how the matter appeared to Keats. Again we are in that world we have already visited. What *is* its peculiar quality? We have said that within it, we are always conscious of two things. First, that the way in which the poet has seen and felt the experience is different from that in which the ordinary man sees and feels experience. It is different, first of all, because instead of being a diffused and general impression of loosely related objects and events, it is a synthesis, in which whatever is significant and eternal in the experience is present, and from which whatever is insignificant and temporal has been excluded. The actual scene and the actual sequence of events in it have been excluded, but the heart and core of its emotional reality to the poet has been seized upon by some mysterious power, revealed in all its riches, and unified into a splendid isolation. And this revelation is made in a particular way. It is not achieved by analysis or argument or statement or description. It is created directly by the poetic vision, and the essence of the poetic vision is that it embodies itself always in the form of symbols. In one complete act of apprehension, Keats embodies the heart and core of that experience with Cowden Clarke into the central symbol of a voyage of discovery. He at once challenges our attention and raises the pitch of the experience which we are to share to a different level, by the first line:

> *Much have I travell'd in the realms of gold.*

At once we are far away from Mr. Alsager and his masterly conduct of the money-market department in the London *Times:* from Cowden Clarke, too, and the very slightly patronizing way in which he pointed out the finest passages to his young friend. Reading Homer is no longer concerned with a certain copy of the book in a particular time and place. It is part of the adventures of the poet's personality in the whole world of books.

At once, too, we become conscious of the second great difference between the world of poetry and the world of statement. *The words are different.* Just as the poet has seen and felt the experience in a special way, so he uses his medium of interpreting and communicating the experience in a special way. Words are no longer merely the means of *conveying* facts. They are concerned to *suggest the quality* of those facts. They are no longer *practical*: they are *evocative.* Here they are required to communicate the quality which the poet discerns in his beloved world of books and reading, and all the rich-ness, the rareness, the colour, the sovereign power which dwell for him in the atmosphere of that world, he in-carnates in the two words he uses to suggest it, *the realms of gold.* All its associations with romance, with poetry, with the medieval flavour he loved, with Greek myth, and Apollo, the Greek God of song and sunrise, he packed into his description of the islands in those golden realms, *which bards in fealty to Apollo hold.*

And now the central symbol of the poet's voyage of discovery among books is enlarged and enriched by the creation of new images and a swelling and intensification of the emotion. The atmosphere of excited exploration is changed to that of triumphant achievement. Words loaded with atmosphere and colour give place to those clear direct monosyllables, *I heard Chapman speak out loud and bold.* And finally we are swept forward to see and feel those two marvellous symbols of the living spirit of discovery, which form the sestet of the sonnet. As we read of Cortez, too, the unity of the imagery throughout is strengthened by the echo of the 'realms of gold' in the first line. For the realms of gold, besides being Keats's creation of a name for the world of reading, is the literal translation of 'el dorado', the mythical land the conquistadors set out to find, and the greatest of the conquistadors was Cortez.[1]

By that act of apprehension, indeed, which the poetic vision of Keats achieved from all the materials which that experience presented to it, and by the language which gave it form, is created in fourteen lines of verse, a new world. A world in which the original experience he shared with Cowden Clarke—the actual experience of spending a night in reading a book, no longer exists. Instead of a scene in which the actors were Charles Cowden Clarke and John Keats and Mr. Alsager's copy of Chapman's Homer, there is a world, contained within the confines of an abstract shape of fourteen lines, in which romance and Eldorado and Greece, Homer and Apollo, Chapman and Cortez and the poet himself, Darien and the empyrean, all harmonize into one exquisite unity of being.

4.

How poetry comes to the poet is a mystery. The idea of the Muse is an obvious symbol of the fact which all creators have felt to be true—that inspiration is a reality. Something of what Mozart describes in one of his letters happens to every artist.

'When I am feeling well and in good humour... thoughts come in swarms and with marvellous ease... Once I catch my air, another comes soon to join the first, according to the requirements of the whole composition... Then my mind kindles—the work grows—I keep hearing it and bring it out more and more clearly, and the composition ends by being completely executed in my mind, however long it may be.'

[1] See *Studies in Keats.* J. Middleton Murry.

Something, which is usually called the imagination, comes to the poet which not only sharpens and intensifies all the faculties he shares in common with his fellow men, but creates a new function of his mind which they do not possess. It is a function which enables the poet to release his imprisoned and chafing vitality in the particular form it needs to take, that is, in the poetic act. Keats describes himself, when the creative passion is upon him, as living under an everlasting restraint, never relieved except when he was composing. Wordsworth calls it a passion and a power, by which we 'see into the life of things'. This must be what Keats means, too, when he declares that a poet is the most unpoetical thing in existence because he has no identity, he is continually filling some other body, and thus partaking of experience in unfamiliar modes. When he is possessed by the need to write poetry, the poet only exists with great difficulty and distress in the actual and factual world about him. His mind is not functioning in that world: he is a stranger there. For the passion and the power generate in him 'unknown modes of being'. And it is this sense of unknown modes of being, this faculty for revealing things to the mind in relationships which are hidden in normal experience, which is the innermost secret of poetic genius. The poet, as Wordsworth again says, rejoices more than other men in the spirit of life which is in him, but besides the passion of perception which that joy brings him, is that particular power of synthesizing perceptions which other men lack: that power of conceiving experiences in the terms of something else; of seizing and communicating analogies; of creating symbol, image, metaphor; and of associating in this way different levels and kinds of experience (such as exploring and Homer and astronomy and reading books), so that their conjunction, by some mysterious intellectual and emotional chemistry, creates a new quality of experience, a new 'mode of being' which was not there before, and which is unlike anything else.

The working of this power is a mystery. It remains a mystery even when its results have been minutely examined. For instance, it so happens that we have the actual clues to all the associations on which the creative passion of Keats seized, and on which it worked when he was composing the famous sonnet. We can guess why it was that Homer and astronomy and Cortez and Darien thronged his mind together,[1] and it is possible to work out in a small way the same process which has already been recreated so brilliantly by J. Livingston Lowes in regard to *The Ancient Mariner* and *Kubla Khan.*

As Keats walked home through the quiet streets, with the stars fading out into the dawn, he may well have had his imagination kindled to an image of 'a watcher of the skies', but this may have been helped by a particular memory of the past. A few years before, when Keats had left school, he had won a prize. It was an introduction to astronomy by a man called Bonnycastle. One of the chapters is called 'Of the new Planets and other discoveries'. The author was fond of lightening his discourses with passages from the poets, and one of these passages was definitely one of those 'famousest passages' from Homer (in Pope's translation) which Cowden Clarke mentions—the shipwreck of Ulysses in the fifth book. He said Keats gave one of his 'delighted stares' as they read the description together—evidently remembering the stilted version of it quoted by Bonnycastle. And so we get the image of the poet as he discovers the 'demesne' of Homer:

> like some watcher of the skies
> When a new planet swims into his ken.

[1] See *Essays and Studies of the English Association*—vol. XVI, for a much fuller account of this.

We can trace, too, something of the working of Keats's mind as it found the famous simile of Cortez and Darien. It is a recollection from a passage in Robertson's *History of America*. The associations of that evening must have made Keats re-live in memory much of his school-days at Enfield. The headmaster of the school was Cowden Clarke's father; the Bonnycastle was a school prize, Keats and Cowden Clarke had made friends over poetry, and we have his direct testimony that Robertson's *History* was one of Keats's favorite books in the school library. It was a small jump, as his mind busied itself with ideas of books and discoveries, from Bonnycastle and astronomy, to Robertson and Darien. In that book he had read

'The isthmus of Darien is not above sixty miles in breadth, but this neck of land . . . is stretched by a chain of lofty mountains . . . which render it a barrier of solidity sufficient to resist the impulses of two opposite oceans. . . .

'At length the Indians assured them, that from the top of the next mountain they should discover the ocean which was the object of their wishes. When, with infinite toil, they had climbed up the greater part of that steep ascent, Balboa commanded his men to halt, and advanced alone to the summit, that he might be the first who should enjoy a spectacle which he had so long desired. As soon as he beheld the South Sea stretching in endless prospect below him, he fell on his knees, and lifting up his hands to Heaven, returned thanks to God. . . . His followers, observing his transports of joy, rushed forward to join in his wonder, exultation and gratitude.'

Why Keats confused Cortez and Balboa we do not know, but we can make a guess. It may have been that immediately before the passage in Robertson of Balboa discovering the Pacific, is a description of a Spanish expedition in which Cortez figures: or it may have been that, as we know from Leigh Hunt, Keats had seen the portrait of Cortez by Titian, and had been greatly impressed by the eyes—the 'eagle eyes' which appeared in the later version of the poem.

The only other change Keats made was to alter the line '*Yet did I never judge what men could mean*' to '*Yet did I never breathe its pure serene*', an echo from Dante which definitely links with the idea of the empyrean and the watcher of the skies.

The picture of Cortez' men owed something to *The Rape of Lucrece:*

> Enchanted Tarquin answers with surmise
> In silent wonder of still gazing eyes.

5.

HERE we can catch a glimpse of the poetic process; of the unifying harmonizing power over material which the poet possesses. A poem is a synthesis of memoried impressions, which the average liver of life leaves in their original chaotic state. 'Life is like a blind and limitless expanse of sky, for ever dividing into tiny drops of circumstance that rain down, thick and fast, a ceaseless, meaningless drip. Art is like the dauntless plastic force that builds up stubborn amorphous substance cell by cell into the frail geometry of a shell.' Into the deep well of our subconscious memory go all the impressions and reminiscences and facts which fall upon our minds and senses and emotions. And there in general they lie, a huddled sleeping company; or they come out straggling and inchoate, the mere tricks of disconnected association. But the poet, with the fire of his imagination, reminds these scraps of memoried litter into new-welded living form, pouring them into a fresh mould, and stamping them with the new bright impress of his own vitality. Poetry and life differ, just as coal and diamonds differ, though the basis of both is exactly the same substance.

The poet remains a man as other men. He is not a mixture of a prophet, a seer, a priest and a medicine man. He may be any manner of man: as moral as Tennyson, as pagan as Keats; as classic as Housman, as romantic as Swinburne; as optimistic as Browning, as pessimistic as Hardy; as mystic as Blake, as practical as Pope; as subtle as de la Mare, as simple as Herrick. The experience he uses as a starting point may be anything: a story, a mood, a moment, an incident, a character, a comment. It may be high or low, grave or gay, steady or fleeting. But whatever it is, it will begin by stirring within him that ferment of excitement, that mysterious working of the glands or the nerve centres or whatever it is which we call inspiration. The sense of inspiration itself is incommunicable. That passion of 'burning with mental bliss' as a modern poet has called it, cannot be transferred, any more than a love poem can communicate the passion of love. The communicable part of the experience, the part with which criticism can concern itself, is that which can be, and is, embodied in words. *Poetry is a special use of words.*

6.

OBVIOUSLY, poetry is impossible without words. A dumb poet, a mute inglorious Milton, is a contradiction in terms. We may say loosely that a sunset or a pretty woman is a perfect poem, but we mean nothing by that except that we consider the sunset or the woman a beautiful thing. We may say of someone that he or she has the mind of a poet, but all we mean is that he or she is sensitive or subtle above the average. Poetry is the communication of experience through the medium of lan-

guage used in a certain way. We have already said that
the poet's use of language is evocative, not practical. The
poet does not find words to project the 'plain sense' of
the experience he wishes to express. He finds words to
express the whole infinitely complicated business of its
happening *to him*: the emotions it aroused, the sensa-
tions which accompanied it, the atmosphere it created,
the memories it awakened. And that not vaguely, but
the exact tone and shade and composition of all these
things. This evocative, suggestive value of words is an
essential of poetry, but it is a quality which poetry shares
with a great deal of prose. When we read in Dorothy
Wordsworth's journal that the daffodils 'tossed and
reeled and danced and seemed as if they verily laughed
in the wind', there is no distinction between the way in
which she uses language to express her experience, and
the way her brother uses it to express the same experience
as he saw and felt it.

> I wandered lonely as a cloud
> That floats on high o'er vales and hills,
> When all at once I saw a crowd,
> A host, of golden daffodils;
> Beside the lake, beneath the trees,
> Fluttering and dancing in the breeze.
>
> Continuous as the stars that shine
> And twinkle on the milky way,
> They stretched in never-ending line
> Along the margin of a bay:
> Ten thousand saw I at a glance,
> Tossing their heads in sprightly dance.
>
> The waves beside them danced; but they
> Out-did the sparkling waves in glee:
> A poet could not but be gay,
> In such a jocund company:
> I gazed—and gazed—but little thought
> What wealth the show to me had brought:

For oft, when on my couch I lie
In vacant or in pensive mood,
They flash upon that inward eye
Which is the bliss of solitude;
And then my heart with pleasure fills,
And dances with the daffodils.

In the same way a great deal of the prose of Virginia Woolf is the prose of a poet. That is, the way she apprehends experience, both in its intensity and its subtlety, and in the power she has of revealing 'unknown modes of being' through her creation and association of images, is the way of a poet. Her 'thought' is 'poetic thought': but her medium of expression is prose. There is one essential difference in the use of language which is present in Keats's sonnet and in Wordsworth's poem, which is absent from Dorothy Wordsworth and Virginia Woolf. It is the element of *sustained, unified organic rhythm*. This sounds an ugly and clumsy description, perhaps, but it is not possible to simplify it. Prose has its rhythms no less than verse, so to say that poetry is rhythmical language is not enough. It is not enough to say that poetry possesses a regular rhythm, since much free verse does not possess it, and is none the less poetry for that. It is a rhythm which only arises when experience has been conceived in a certain way, at a certain pitch and with a certain tension. Poetry is a use of words which creates a living organism, which builds up a unique harmony of being in which this rhythm—both in its larger sense of the general design, movement or flow of the poetic thought, and in its more limited sense of the sound pattern—is always an essential and intrinsic part.

WHAT POETRY DOES

I.

Poetry does many things, for it affects the reader at many different levels of his consciousness. Almost every poem is formed of many associations, drawn from many planes of experience, and it turns therefore many facets to criticism. Just as one person may enjoy *Hamlet* because it is excellent melodrama, and another person may enjoy it for its characterization, and another person may enjoy it for its poetry; so one reader may enjoy poetry for its subject matter, and another for its verbal music, and another as a mental tonic. We crave different things of poetry at different times. There must always be moods when F. L. Lucas's poem *To the Graces* seems the answer to all the problems of appreciation; when we want nothing but those 'little things that grow not less.'

> Your quiet altar after all was best,
>   Fair sisters. Louder faiths grow cold.
> Not you forged earth's foundations: but you blessed
>   What flowers her deserts hold.
> Not yours alone is power that does not perish;
> But yours is Youth. Only what your hands cherish,
>   Grows not old.
>
> Not yours the mouths that justify God's ways,
>   By whom the depths of Hell are sung;
> Deathless they seem, yet aged. Green their bays,
>   Yet time has touched their tongue.

But Sappho's grace, La Fontaine's quiet laughter,
The lilt of Herrick—these heed no hereafter,
   These are young.

All else turns vanity: but yours the day
   Of little things that grow not less.
Our moments fly—enough if on their way
   You lent them loveliness.
Alone of gods, you lie not; yours no Heaven
That totters in the clouds—what you have given,
   We possess.

Or we may long for that poetry which sings of delight in sensuous and temporal and purely physical and human things for their own sweet and lovely sakes.

THE NIGHT-PIECE: TO JULIA

Her eyes the glow-worm lend thee,
The shooting stars attend thee;
   And the elves also,
   Whose little eyes glow
Like the sparks of fire, befriend thee.

No will-o'-the-wisp mislight thee,
Nor snake or slow-worm bite thee;
   But on, on thy way
   Not making a stay,
Since ghost there's none to affright thee.

Let not the dark thee cumber:
What though the moon does slumber?
   The stars of the night
   Will lend thee their light
Like tapers clear without number.

Then, Julia, let me woo thee,
Thus, thus to come unto me;
   And when I shall meet
   Thy silv'ry feet
My soul I'll pour into thee.

(Robert Herrick)

THE GARDEN

·   ·   ·   ·   ·   ·

What wondrous life is this I lead!
Ripe apples drop about my head;
The luscious clusters of the vine
Upon my mouth do crush their wine;
The nectarine and curious peach,
Into my hands themselves do reach;
Stumbling on melons, as I pass,
Insnar'd with flowers, I fall on grass.

Meanwhile the mind, from pleasure less,
Withdraws into its happiness;
The mind, that ocean where each kind
Does straight its own resemblance find;
Yet it creates, transcending these,
Far other worlds, and other seas;
Annihilating all that's made
To a green thought in a green shade.

Here at the fountain's sliding foot,
Or at some fruit-tree's mossy root,
Casting the body's vest aside
My soul into the boughs does glide:
There like a bird it sits, and sings,
Then whets, and combs its silver wings;
And, till prepar'd for longer flight,
Waves in its plumes the various light.

·   ·   ·   ·   ·   ·

(Andrew Marvell)

A BIRTHDAY

My heart is like a singing bird
Whose nest is in a water'd shoot;
My heart is like an apple-tree
Whose boughs are bent with thick-set fruit;

My heart is like a rainbow shell
That paddles in a halcyon sea;
My heart is gladder than all these
Because my love is come to me.

Raise me a daïs of silk and down;
Hang it with vair and purple dyes;
Carve it in doves and pomegranates,
And peacocks with a hundred eyes;
Work it in gold and silver grapes,
In leaves and silver fleurs-de-lys
Because the birthday of my life
Is come, my love is come to me.

(Christina Rossetti)

Or we may feel in tune with something quite different.

Say not the struggle nought availeth,
The labour and the wounds are vain,
The enemy faints not, nor faileth,
And as things have been they remain.

If hopes were dupes, fears may be liars;
It may be, in yon smoke conceal'd
Your comrades chase e'en now the fliers,
And, but for you, possess the field.

For while the tired waves, vainly breaking,
Seem here no painful inch to gain,
Far back, through creeks and inlets making,
Comes silent, flooding in, the main.

And not by eastern windows only,
When daylight comes, comes in the light;
In front the sun climbs slow, how slowly!
But westward, look, the land is bright!

(Arthur Hugh Clough)

2.

THIS last illustration represents very fairly a type of
poetry which has, perhaps, more admirers than any
other. It is so human and appealing. It is written with
such sympathetic understanding of the common human
lot; of the common human longings and vague aspira-
tions and baffled questionings, and of those emotional
moments of comfort when the eternal riddle seems
solved for a time. It is poetry concerned with all the
ultimate human values about which we feel poetry some-
how ought to be concerned. For very, very deeply rooted
in most of us is the tradition of generations of readers
who have been convinced that the main function of
poetry is to teach, and of generations of critics who have
declared that poetry should be serious and earnest and
dignified and uplifting; that it should be related to con-
ceptions of the Good, the Beautiful and the True, and
be shot through with transcendental ideas and a certain
misty idealism. So that even Wordsworth, who was so
passionately interested in the mystery of poetic creation,
nevertheless declared that the aim of his poetry was 'to
teach the young and the gracious of every age, to see, to
think, and feel, and therefore, to become more actively
and securely virtuous.' In all its history, indeed, poetry
has been so often commended, even by its most devoted
lovers, for something not really essential to it at all; just
as doctors recommend dancing for exercise, or garden-
ing because bending and rising braces up the abdominal
muscles. There are still multitudes of people who go to
poetry for—or at least take from poetry nothing but—
its 'message'. They find it the Polonius of the arts, a
mine of useful and bracing quotations: 'A man's reach
should exceed his grasp, or what's a heaven for?' 'They
also serve who only stand and wait.' ' 'Tis better to have
loved and lost . . . , and so on. Now there are many

times when all of us can feel sustained and comforted by quotations, and there is no need to be superior about the value of mottoes on the wall. We are all men and women after all, and one of the great secrets of poetry is that it understands our common human nature so well. And just as it is one of the pleasures of dancing and gardening that they are a tonic to the circulation, so it is one of the pleasures of poetry that a great deal of it is a tonic to the moral nature. But the real value of poetry is very much wider than its moral stimulus, just as the value of dancing and gardening is very much wider than its stimulus to the muscles, and it is our aim in this book to try and discover what that value is.

At the opposite extreme from the purely ethical type of criticism is that which is associated with its first formulator, Oscar Wilde. In his famous preface to *Intentions* Wilde combated the view that literature should have a moral aim, by an entirely new credo:

'There is no such thing as a moral or an immoral book. Books are well written or badly written. That is all.

No artist has ethical sympathies. An ethical sympathy in an artist is an unpardonable mannerism of style.

They are the elect to whom beautiful things mean only Beauty.

All Art is quite useless.'

It was Oscar Wilde indeed who popularized the theory that there is a certain kind of emotion—the aesthetic emotion—which can be isolated, and that the values of poetry dwell in this emotion and can therefore be isolated too. It is the theory which assumes that the experiences of poetry and the experiences of life can, and should be, kept in water-tight compartments, and that any criticism of poetry in terms of life is invalid.

Perhaps the best way to meet this theory is to go to

poetry itself, and to find poems which flatly contradict the statement that no artist has ethical sympathies: poems which are poetry of a high order, and in which it is utterly impossible to divorce the words in which the thought and feeling are expressed, from the ethical significance of that thought and feeling.

> Let me not to the marriage of true minds
> Admit impediments. Love is not love
> Which alters when it alteration finds,
> Or bends with the remover to remove:
> O, no! it is an ever-fixed mark,
> That looks on tempests and is never shaken;
> It is the star to every wand'ring bark,
> Whose worth's unknown, although his height be taken.
> Love's not time's fool, though rosy lips and cheeks
> Within his bending sickle's compass come;
> Love alters not with his brief hours and weeks,
> But bears it out even to the edge of doom.
> > If this be error and upon me proved,
> > I never writ, nor no man ever loved.

> (William Shakespeare)

THE LAST WORD

> Creep into thy narrow bed,
> Creep, and let no more be said!
> Vain thy onset! all stands fast;
> Thou thyself must break at last.

> Let the long contention cease!
> Geese are swans, and swans are geese.
> Let them have it how they will!
> Thou art tired; best be still!

> They out-talk'd thee, hiss'd thee, tore thee.
> Better men fared thus before thee;
> Fired their ringing shot and pass'd,
> Hotly charged—and broke at last.

Charge once more, then, and be dumb!
Let the victors, when they come,
When the forts of folly fall,
Find thy body by the wall.

(Matthew Arnold)

UPHILL

Does the road wind uphill all the way?
　Yes, to the very end.
Will the day's journey take the whole long day?
　From morn to night, my friend.

But is there for the night a resting place?
　A roof for when the slow, dark hours begin.
May not the darkness hide it from my face?
　You cannot miss that inn.

Shall I meet other wayfarers at night?
　Those who have gone before.
Then must I knock, or call when just in sight?
　They will not keep you waiting at the door.

Shall I find comfort, travel-sore and weak?
　Of labour you shall find the sum.
Will there be beds for me and all who seek?
　Yea, beds for all who come.

(Christina Rossetti)

LOVE

Love bade me welcome; yet my soul drew back,
　　Guilty of dust and sin.
But quick-ey'd Love, observing me grow slack
　　From my first entrance in,
Drew nearer to me, sweetly questioning,
　　If I lack'd any thing.

A guest, I answer'd, worthy to be here:
        Love said, you shall be he.
I the unkind, ungrateful? Oh my dear,
        I cannot look on thee.
Love took my hand, and smiling did reply,
        Who made the eyes but I?

Truth Lord, but I have marr'd them: let my shame
        Go where it doth deserve.
And know you not, says Love, who bore the blame?
        My dear, then I will serve.
You must sit down, says Love, and taste my meat:
        So I did sit and eat.

(George Herbert)

It is indeed impossible to speak of poetry in the terms
of a 'pure' art. Its experiences and its values are more
complex than those of any other art, for both its subject
matter and its medium are inextricably involved with
the bosoms and business of men. Its material is human
life, and its medium is the medium by means of which
we live our lives—human speech. This makes it a sheer
impossibility to keep poetry and life in water-tight com-
partments. We have all felt about poetry as Lady Ann
Clifford wrote about it in the seventeenth century: 'If I
had not excellent Chaucer's book here to comfort me,
I were in a pitiable case, having as many troubles as I
have here, but, when I read in that, I scorn and make
light of them all, and a little part of that beauteous spirit
infuses itself in me.' Poetry cannot exist in a detached
art-world of its own if it springs from the emotions and
sensations which are common to us all. And it does. Do
we not have the same feelings towards the subjects of
youth and old age, towards human cruelty and human
pity, when we read *King Lear* as when we meet similar
facts in real life? Does not our own intimate sense of
loss spring to life in *In Memoriam*?; our own joy in *My*

heart is like a singing bird? It is true that the actual
emotions felt in a poetic experience are very much
diluted and enfeebled compared with direct emotional
experience in life. They correspond to remembered emo-
tions. They are evoked, too, through the medium of
language, not of life itself, which makes their effect dif-
ferent. Something is taken away from the effect, and
something is added to it. But in spite of this, the emo-
tions remain the same emotions: they are different in
degree, not in kind. It is impossible, as I. A. Richards
points out, to keep the theory and the fact of poetry
apart, to banish certain parts of our consciousness from
participation in the appreciation of poetry. 'There is no
such gulf between poetry and life as over-literary per-
sons sometimes suppose. There is no gap between our
everyday emotional life and the material for poetry.
The verbal expression of this life, at its finest, is forced
to use the technique of poetry; that is the only essential
difference.'

3.

WHAT then *does* poetry do, what *is* its value? There
have never been lacking lovers of poetry who have
praised it in the language of hyperbole. 'It acts,' says
Shelley, 'in a divine and unapprehended manner, beyond
and above consciousness.' 'Through poetry,' says Jacques
Maritain, 'the soul catches a glimpse of splendours be-
yond the tomb.' But surely it should be possible to
analyze its experiences in more rational and mundane
terms while losing none of its sense of glory. Can we
not be more lucid and intelligible about the effects of
poetry? W. B. Yeats says that poetry would not move us
'if our thought did not rush out to the edges of our
flesh. Poetry,' he declares, 'bids us touch and taste and
hear and see the world, and shrink from all that is of the
brain only, from all that is not a fountain jetting from

the entire hopes, memories and sensations of the body.'
This is one of the great values of poetry: its invigoration
of the whole consciousness. Why is it that poetry can
make us feel as if the sea itself flowed in our veins, as
if we are clothed with the heavens and crowned with the
stars? It is not because we glimpse splendours beyond the
tomb, or pass beyond and above consciousness, it is that
we discover this world, and the heights and depths and
infinite variety of the experiences of this world. They
include everything from the vision of eternity to a
louse; from the glory of God to the lesser celandine.
Sometimes we touch a mode of experience utterly be-
yond our own, sometimes it is a remembering, sometimes
it is a matching of our mood of the moment. Each will
present us with a different facet of our own conscious-
ness, and each in its way will add to the riches of our
experience.

It is not by telling us *about* life that poetry enriches it;
it is by *being* life. As Browning shows us, the poet does
not analyze and explain what a rose is. He is one who

> With a 'look you!' vents a brace of rhymes,
> And in there breaks the sudden rose itself,
> Over us, under, round us every side,
> Buries us with a glory, young once more,
> Pouring heaven into this shut house of life.

To love experience for its own sake, to want to get as
much of it, and as great variety of it as we can, is a
natural human instinct; and because the poet pricks our
dull and drowsy feelings and senses awake by the keen-
ness of his own perceptions, we feel quickened and re-
freshed by the reading of poetry. It is an emotional and
mental tonic, as well as a moral tonic. But poetry does
more than merely intensify all our perceptions. As we
have said before, the poet's inspiration, what goes on in
his mind when he receives the actual experience, and

how it works within his mind, like yeast in dough, be-
tween the reception of the stimulus (the experience) and
the response (the writing of the poem), we do not know.
What we do know, what is obvious, is that the writing
of the poem is a certain 'ordering' of the experience.
I. A. Richards, who has given the fullest and most
interesting account of the psychological processes of
poetry, uses the word 'organize' to describe the relation
of the poet to his material, because, he points out, the
word organize does not only have the practical sugges-
tion of putting in good order, but implies also that vital
spirit of coherence which distinguishes the organic from
the inorganic. So that when we say the poet *organizes*
his experience, we mean both that he puts it in order,
and gives it a life of its own.

It is not a very alluring word to use of poetry, and
yet to conceive of poetry as organized vitality, with this
double sense behind it, does give the key to what is the
main function of poetry, to what it does to us over and
above stimulating us to a keener sense of living. *It gives
us a special kind of living*. We have already seen some-
thing of what this independent life which dwells in
poetry is. The material of poetry is human experience
but it is human experience apprehended and re-created
in a special way. It does not analyze life, or reason about
life or merely describe life: 'it bids us touch and taste
and hear and see the world, and shrink from all that is
of the brain only, from all that is not a fountain jetting
from the entire hopes, memories and sensations of the
body.' The poetic vision fuses the whole intellectual,
moral, emotional and physical natures of man. It does
not only stimulate, it also harmonizes. Along with the
sense of excitement which it communicates, goes a sense
of fulfilment. This is, indeed, what actually happens
biologically. There is a stirring up of responses followed

by a co-ordination of them; an elaborated nervous circuit, followed by an appropriate adaptive reaction.

Now it is one natural function of the organism to seek experience. From the flatworm to ourselves, organic life possesses curiosity. And it is another natural function of the organism to co-ordinate. None of us could live for a moment or perform the simplest movement without a most intricate ordering of the nervous system. When we pass from the simple actions of practical living to the complicated activities which determine what *kind* of life we shall live, the arrangements involved in the nervous system are of quite incalculable complexity. Daily we become the unconscious and conscious battlefield of vast hordes of warring impulses, and our life is one long effort of conscious and unconscious adjustment.

These efforts are all directed towards freedom and fullness of life, self-completion, or perfection of co-ordination among all the myriad claims of our intellectual, emotional, moral and physical being. It is the nature of the healthy organism to delight in fine coordination. We all know the sense of satisfaction, of fulfilment, which comes from more than usual order or coherence of any kind. It may be purely intellectual— a lucid scientific exposition, for example; or a complex organization of human material towards practical efficiency, as in a ship's crew, or a big business; or it may be emotional. We all know people, very often people of no education at all, whose human, emotional nature seems to possess perfect control, balance and beauty. And this sense of satisfaction in the presence of successful co-ordination, is matched by a sense of frustration and disharmony when we meet disorder or muddle, from the discomfort we feel at the blurred presentation of a simple argument, up to the passion of rebellion which can seize us at the warpings and distortions of the human soul. 'The wrong of unshapely things is a wrong too great to be told.' Man is an ordering animal. Civilization is order imposed on disorder, cosmos created from chaos.

But individuals differ widely in their capacities and limitations in co-ordinating power, and each individual varies widely within his own scope. We all know that there are special times and special experiences and the influence of special individuals which produce a condition in us when we feel ourselves to be harmonious and at one. The psychologists tell us that these conditions of easy adjustment and ordered vitality occur at times when there is the minimum of suppression and sacrifice and frustration among our nervous activities; when the minimum of effort is needed to hold the balance of warring forces; when the maximum number of our total claims is being satisfied; when, in a word, we are most fully *alive*. At such times we are conscious of a general heightening and sharpening of sensibility; we recognize a quickness and fineness of response in ourselves of which we are not generally capable; and we instinctively feel and know that the times when we attain to this finely poised equilibrium are the hours of greatest value in our lives.

The causes which create such moments vary with each individual and within each individual. It may be human love, or any of the myriad adjustments of sympathetic human relationships. It may be religious ecstasy or contemplation; it may be communion with nature, or the creation of art; the passionate pursuit of what Sir Philip Sidney calls 'the tougher knowledges', or the thrill of physical adventure. Or it may be the reading of poetry. For in poetry that special harmony of vision created by the poet is communicated to the reader (if he be capable of receiving it). He too 'apprehends'. He recognizes that profound satisfaction which is the unmistakable symptom of a more perfect co-ordination of his whole nervous potentialities. It brings him finer and wider responses, or in more old-fashioned language, increased fullness of life, greater riches of the senses, the mind and the spirit.

4.

HERE is the moral value of poetry, which is at the same time the reason for the delight of poetry. They are inseparable. If we love poetry, it vitalizes and harmonizes and enlarges our whole being. It is not only a revelation of spiritual values, but of *all* values, moral as well as intellectual, emotional and sensuous. As for the question of the direct ethical influence of poetry, it must, of course, vary enormously according to the temperament of the reader. Sir Philip Sidney said, 'I have known men, and that even with reading *Amadis de Gaul* (which God knoweth wanteth much of a perfect Poesie) have found their hearts moved to the exercise of courtesie, liberalitie and especially courage.' But the over-simple reader who uses poetry as a moral tonic loses as much of the reality of poetry as the over-sophisticated reader who is determined to regard ethical interests as a mere mannerism of style. The ultimate end of poetry is neither to be didactic or not to be didactic. It is to be poetry. It is impossible to exclude ethical questions from poetry, simply because they are an essential part of life and are therefore deeply involved in any ordering of the average reader's mind. Matthew Arnold was expressing a general truth and not a Victorian dogma when he said 'a poetry of revolt against moral ideas is a poetry of revolt against life; a poetry of indifference towards moral ideas is a poetry of indifference towards life.' Though we may have rebelled sincerely from the Victorian identification of the *whole* value of life with the purely ethical values in it, we are still all moralists at heart. If we do not hold one set of moral attitudes, it is because we hold another.

We cannot escape from ethical standards. Hence, we could certainly never attain to any satisfying harmony of our impulses if so important a part of us as our moral nature were not with us in poetry, or at least, not against us. There is, of course, a vast body of poetry in which questions of belief or conduct never arise at all. A masterpiece such as Keats's *Ode to a Nightingale,* for instance, has nothing ethical in it whatever. Or again, there is a large body of poetry—mainly religious verse—where the beliefs may be indifferent to us, but to which we can give 'emotional' as opposed to 'intellectual' belief, if the poetry itself takes us captive. But I know of no fine poetry which concerns itself with questions of human conduct (except, of course, incidentally in drama) where the traditional code of honourable people is not implicit, or which comes to any ethical conclusions about life which the common reader would feel to be 'immoral'— such as, for instance, the conclusion that cruelty, or selfishness, or disloyalty, or cowardice were really admirable qualities. The jar of such an idea would jangle our responses too completely out of tune to achieve the co-ordinating effect of poetry, however perfect the form in which it were expressed.

And to the vast majority of readers, in the greatest poetry, that is, the poetry which comprehends most in its scope—the poetry, which, to English-speaking peoples, culminates in the tragedies of Shakespeare—it is surely true, as critics and readers all down the ages have insisted, that, inevitably, a great part of the total effect is achieved by the actual direct satisfaction such poetry gives to our sense of the moral structure of human life. Not, needless to say, that it gives satisfacton to the idea that virtue triumphs, but to the conviction that the great moral qualities are the imperishable and immortal human values in a world of mortality. Pater perhaps expresses it best in his distinction between good art—which depends on the question of style alone—and great art.

'It is on the quality of the matter it informs and controls, its compass, its variety, its alliance to great ends, or the depth of the work of revolt, or the largeness of hope in it, that the greatness of literary art depends. . . . Given the conditions I have tried to explain as constituting good art;—then, if it be devoted further to the increase of men's happiness, to the redemption of the oppressed, or the enlargement of our sympathies with each other, or to such presentment of new or old truth about ourselves and our relation to the world as may ennoble and fortify us in our sojourn here . . . it will be also great art.'

THE READER

I.

THE TWO POETS

Whose is the speech
That moves the voices of this lonely beech?
Out of the long west did this wild wind come—
Oh strong and silent! And the tree was dumb,
Ready and dumb, until
The dumb gale struck it on the darkened hill.

Two memories,
Two powers, two promises, two silences
Closed in this cry, closed in these thousand leaves
Articulate. This sudden hour retrieves
The purpose of the past,
Separate, apart,—embraced, embraced at last.

'Whose is the word?
Is it I that spake? Is it thou? Is it I that heard?'
'Thine earth was solitary, yet I found thee!'
'Thy sky was pathless, but I caught, I bound thee,
Thou visitant divine.'
'O thou my Voice, the word was thine.' 'Was thine.'

(Alice Meynell)

The value of a stimulus depends on the quality of its response: and the value of poetry to the reader depends on the quality of that reader.

Through the medium of language the poet communicates all he can of the whole vitality of his experience, and it is what happens to the reader during that act of communication which conditions his judgment of the poem. If it pleases the reader, if, as we saw earlier, it co-ordinates his responses, he will say of it that it is a good or a beautiful poem. Now what does he mean when he says that?

There is a quotation from a Japanese writer of the fourteenth century which is apposite and helpful: 'What standard have we,' he says, 'to discern good from bad?' And the answer returned is: 'We can only take what suits the need of the moment and call it good.'

The acceptance of this answer involves the acceptance of that view of aesthetics which holds as its central doc-trine that 'beauty' cannot be spoken of (as it usually *is* spoken of) as if it dwelt entirely in the work of art. That, in fact, when the reader says that a poem is good or beautiful, what he really means is that it has a par-ticular effect upon *him*: that beauty is an experience. It cannot be that there is some peculiar quality which can be isolated and defined in the poem—labelled 'good-ness' or 'beauty', because the next reader may come along and declare that it is a very bad poem. When we speak of poems of the past as beautiful, what we really mean is that the vast majority of people whom we con-sider best qualified to judge have found that those poems affect them in a similar way—that they 'suit their need' in fact. Poetry can only be judged by the standard of the personality that is judging it. We cannot escape our own limitations. Each reader gets the poetry he deserves. To adapt Coleridge a little and put Beauty in the place of nature:

> O Wordsworth, we receive but what we give
> And in *our* life alone does Beauty live.

Or as Blake says even more succinctly:

> The sun's light when he unfolds it
> Depends on the organ which beholds it.

We all know that sense of blankness when we read a poem highly recommended by some one else—and nothing whatever is communicated to us; and we can compare that feeling with the sense of tingling penetration which follows if we do respond; maybe with a shock of glad surprise, maybe with the slow surge of familiar emotion. In fact we can discuss the *effect* of beauty, or the absence of beauty, but we cannot dogmatize about its *essence*.

2.

As soon as we set about studying the art of receiving experiences through the medium of language, which is the art of enjoying poetry, and the whole object of our quest, we begin to realize the fabulous complications of the adventure. On the one side there is the poet. A being, like all the rest of mankind, on a planet swarming with his fellow creatures, teeming with life, thronged by hordes and herds of his brothers, and yet a being living in an indestructible loneliness. Weaving the intricate pattern of his fate in a concealment only pierced from without by occasional glimpses, like rents in a fog. A being essentially inexplicable and inexpressible, yet struggling passionately to express and explain himself, to convey the unique quality of his human consciousness, of his traffic with the worlds of brain and blood. The earthly symbol he must use to do this, the symbol of language, will be *his* particular selection of words, coloured by *his* personality and by the character of *his* poetic experience. It will further inevitably be influenced by the age he lives in, by his whole social, intellectual and physical environment, and by his acceptance of, or revolt from, tradition.

On the other side there is the reader. He is another isolated individuality, coloured by other experience and environment, belonging very likely to another age and culture and civilization, limited in a hundred ways by radical psychological differences, and the sport of a hundred accidental local influences on his nervous adjustments, such as noise, or health, or mood, or weather.

And the poet's means of communication is limited to one medium only: that of words. Everything which in a direct human relationship can be aided by look, by tone, by gesture, by explanation, is denied to the poet. *Everything* must be in the words—and not words in free, lavish abundance, but words in a particular pattern and arrangement of rhythmical language, which imposes still further limitations.

3.

IT is clear then that the co-operation of the reader must be an active one if he is to 'discover' poetry. And yet the first ideas which that sentence suggests, the ideas of 'getting busy' and concentrating and taking action are the very opposite of what is needed to begin. 'One cannot reach Parnassus except by flying thither': poetry cannot be stormed. We have said that the full appreciation of poetry demands two kinds of experience about it—apprehension and comprehension: and of these by far the most important is apprehension. Now an act of apprehension is the unconscious adjustment of a number of factors into a harmonious whole. At the moment of making it, we do not analyze what has produced this feeling of a harmonious whole, any more than, for example, when we can ride a bicycle we analyze the feeling of being able to ride, into the elements of control and capacity which have produced the feeling. In the same way, we feel we grasp a poem without analyzing that feeling into all the physical and emotional and intellectual elements which have produced it. And no amount of mere logical analysis of the various elements which combine and cohere to create a poem will give us the 'feel' of a poem, unless we have experienced it by apprehension first: just as no amount of analysis of the anatomical, dynamic, and mechanical principles involved will give us the 'feel' of riding a bicycle if we have never experienced it first. 'It has been an old comparison for our urging on—the Beehive,' says Keats, 'however, it seems to me that we should rather be the flower than the bee.... Let us open our leaves like a flower and be passive and receptive ... sap will be given us for meat and dew for drink.'

> Now sleeps the crimson petal, now the white;
>   Nor waves the cypress in the palace walk;
> Nor winks the gold fin in the porphyry font:
> The firefly wakens: waken thou with me.
>
>   Now droops the milk-white peacock like a ghost,
> And like a ghost she glimmers on to me.
>
>   Now lies the Earth all Danaë to the stars,
> And all thy heart lies open unto me.
>
>   Now slides the silent meteor on, and leaves
> A shining furrow, as thy thoughts in me.
>
>   Now folds the lily all her sweetness up,
> And slips into the bosom of the lake:
> So fold thyself, my dearest, thou, and slip
> Into my bosom and be lost in me.
>
> (Alfred Tennyson)

We must first surrender to poetry; abandon our-
selves entirely to the poet while we read, because it is
clear from a consideration of all that his words have to
communicate to us, how impossible it is to read any but
the most trivial verse rapidly or carelessly. Glancing
through a poem, if the poem is worth anything at all,
will tell us little or nothing about it. It is like trying to
judge personality from meeting a person at afternoon
tea. We have got to become as much a part of the poet's
own consciousness as we can, if we are to enjoy fully
and to discriminate and value justly. We have got to be
in a state when we can respond to his experience as a
whole, with the whole of ourselves, and reproduce as
nearly as we can in ourselves, all that the poet suggests
and evokes. We have got to get *into* the poem, not to
stand outside it. If we remain outside it, our tendency
is to give a judgment on what we think the poem *ought*
to be, not on what it is. And so we find Matthew Arnold
blaming Shelley for being 'an ineffectual angel' or Mrs.
Barbauld condemning *The Ancient Mariner* as im-
probable.

This over-intellectual manner of reading, judging it
by the mind only, is one to which all rational and literal-
minded people are specially subject. They skim a poem
once, say, 'I can't see that it means anything' and dis-
miss it: or, on the other hand, they will accept any neat,
logical verses on a familiar subject, as good poetry. This
attitude and type of criticism come from the delusion
that it is what a poem *says* that matters, that is, the part
which can be as easily expressed in prose. It is encour-
aged by the practice in some schools of paraphrasing
poetry, an entirely futile way of trying to teach it. For
a poem *cannot* be expressed in prose. The quality of ex-
perience can only be tasted by getting the same flavour
ourselves upon the emotional palate. The actual sense of

a poem, the thought, the prose 'meaning' plays a very small, though it is a very important part, in the whole business of reading. It is a very important part because, unless we actually grasp the structure and sequence of the ideas and the syntax of the words, we are at a deadlock. We cannot possibly proceed any further in our response. Everything, therefore, springs *from* the subject, but very little is actually in it. Once we have apprehended it, we can begin to read the words *as a poem*: that is, we subordinate reason to impression, thought to a complex stream of feeling, ideas to sensibility. We *live* the words. We subdue our own personality to that of the poet and submerge ourselves in 'a wise passiveness' to the tone and atmosphere and composition of his consciousness.

And curiously enough, instead of this impairing the unity of the reader's personality, it seems to enhance it. It is the story of he that shall lose his life shall find it. A receptive relaxation, an abandonment of the will to the imagination, leaves the reader free to receive all that the poet can give. The poet's vitality kindles his and fans it into flame; his responses are heightened and sensitized, and just as speed assists all physical adjustments, so that we can perform tricks of delicate balance when skating or dancing, which we could not possibly accomplish at rest, or moving slowly, so this heightening of sensibility seems to create a suppleness and fineness of adaptation in the reader, of which he is not normally capable.

Alternatively, the intellectual, rational approach to poetry is like tenseness and rigidity in muscular effort. It at once inhibits free co-ordination, causes a stasis in the nerve centres, and interferes with the harmonizing power which is struggling to work towards greater fullness of life.

4.

IT is helpful to analyze some of the practical difficulties in the way of good reading, exactly as it is helpful to have our physical rigidity illustrated to us. That we should be conscious of such things is the first step towards removing them. Just as poetry is life, and its experiences those of living itself, different in degree but not in kind, everything which interferes with our full appreciation of poetry springs from denial of life, from an unconscious or conscious limiting of our responses, from a hardening of our hearts.

This is at the root of our trouble with poetry which embodies different moral and religious codes from our own. It is easy enough to tell the reader to pay no heed to what the poem *says*, but what if it says something with which morally he disagrees? What if it says something which he regards as intellectually puerile? Since poets are dealing with human experience, and since it is quite impossible to divorce human experience from questions of faith and conduct, it is inevitable that a great deal of poetry shall deal with these matters.

There are many people who prefer that it shouldn't. Particularly in the present day there is a strong preference for what has been called 'pure poetry'—the poetry which is concerned with the sensuous quality of experience, isolated from any moral or intellectual or personal significance it may have—Shakespeare's songs, for example. This is part of the general reaction from the Victorian fashion for ethical poetry, and if we take an illustration of a similar theme treated by a nineteenth century poet (Wordsworth) and a twentieth century poet (W. H. Davies) we shall see at once their difference of approach, the difference between poetry which interprets and criticizes life, and the poetry which expresses life.

My heart leaps up when I behold
  A rainbow in the sky:
So was it when my life began;
So is it now I am a man;
So be it when I shall grow old,
  Or let me die!
The Child is father of the Man;
And I could wish my days to be
Bound each to each by natural piety.

*

Sweet Chance, that led my steps abroad,
Beyond the town, where wild flowers grow—
A rainbow and a cuckoo, Lord!
How rich and great the times are now!
Know, all ye sheep
And cows, that keep
On staring that I stand so long
In grass that's wet from heavy rain—
A rainbow and a cuckoo's song
May never come together again;
May never come
This side the tomb!

But it is impossible to dogmatize about poetry and to say it should be this and shouldn't be that. There is no reason whatever why poetry should not be ethical, just as there is no reason whatever why it should be. There are many poets whose passions are inextricably bound up with their emotional reactions to religious, moral or intellectual concepts, and whose poetry is inevitably an effort to communicate their sense of these realities. But it *is* nevertheless true that there are many readers who find their enjoyment of such poetry interfered with because the opinions of the poets clash with those of themselves.

This is a very real difficulty.

Few people—few readers of poetry anyhow—find

what Coleridge calls 'the willing suspension of disbelief, which constitutes poetic faith' difficult in some matters. There are few readers who cannot enjoy *The Ancient Mariner* or *A Midsummer Night's Dream*. Or again it would be a very rigid social service worker who could not read Burns's *Jolly Beggars* with pleasure, and a very stern agnostic who could not appreciate the simple humanity of this anonymous sixteenth century plea for Christ.

PREPARATIONS

Yet if His Majesty, our sovereign lord,
Should of his own accord
Friendly himself invite,
And say 'I'll be your guest to-morrow night,'
How should we stir ourselves, call and command
All hands to work! 'Let no man idle stand!

'Set me fine Spanish tables in the hall;
See they be fitted all;
Let there be room to eat
And order taken that there want no meat.
See every sconce and candlestick made bright,
That without tapers they may give a light.

'Look to the presence: are the carpets spread,
The dazie o'er the head,
The cushions in the chairs,
And all the candles lighted on the stairs?
Perfume the chambers, and in any case
Let each man give attendance in his place!'

Thus, if a king were coming, would we do;
And 'twere good reason too;
For 'tis a duteous thing
To show all honour to an earthly king,
And after all our travail and our cost,
So he be pleased, to think no labour lost.

But at the coming of the King of Heaven
All's set at six and seven;
We wallow in our sin,
Christ cannot find a chamber in the inn.
We entertain Him always like a stranger,
And, as at first, still lodge Him in the manger.

Nor are there in the present day, probably, many readers who would find their appreciation of *Prometheus Unbound* affected by Shelley's political opinions. But there are quite a number who don't like Milton because of his theology; or who can't read Hardy because of his pessimism; or who are bored by religious verse; or who find modern disillusion repellent; or Wordsworth and Tennyson and Browning and the Victorians in general, mere tiresome preachers.

Now the fact that we find the necessary adjustment to certain poems, which contain things in which we have no personal belief, quite easy, proves that the capacity to ignore such things in poetry is in us, and that all that is necessary is to enlarge that capacity. This is not to deny the inevitable differences of taste. Each of us has (as Virginia Woolf has presented so subtly in *The Waves*) a certain rhythm of personality peculiarly and unchangeably our own, and this in itself must create in each of us a characteristic choice in our response to poetry, and must cause divergences of opinion among even the most discriminating readers. Again it is inevitable that certain poetry should be peculiarly in harmony with certain human modes and moods. We cannot be entirely detached and impersonal about a thing which affects us as intimately as poetry. If we are in love we read love poetry in a special way; if we have lost a loved person we read poems of bereavement in a special way; if we are Catholics we read Catholic poetry in a special way; if we hunt we love poetry about hunting, and so on. In poetic just as in physical nourishment, one man's meat is another man's poison, and it behooves each man to find the meat which serves him best. Healthy spiritual metabolism is every bit as important as healthy physical metabolism, and the harmony of the complete organism depends on both.   Inevitably we shall always respond more flexibly to certain stimuli than to others, but this does not mean that the scope of deliberate self-training in catholicity of experience is not enormous. Intellectual belief *need* never enter at all into the reading of poetry. Emotional belief is all that is needed, and perhaps 'belief' is too strong a word here; say rather, emotional acceptance. If this is cultivated deliberately, by the attitude of surrender to the poetry, it is surprising how soon we find that in fine poetry the question of intellectual acceptance simply does not arise at all, and that we can give a poetic judgment which involves nothing else but the poetic elements in the poem. There is, indeed, a curious sense of pure, detached satisfaction in appreciating poetry with which we disagree intellectually. We leave our own opinions outside the poem, forget entirely to be theologians or philosophers and become pure readers of poetry.

> Batter my heart, three-person'd God; for you
> As yet but knock; breathe, shine, and seek to mend;
> That I may rise, and stand, o'erthrow me, and bend
> Your force to break, blow, burn and make me new.
> I, like an usurp'd town, to another due,
> Labour to admit you, but O, to no end.
> Reason, your viceroy in me, me should defend,
> But is captived, and proves weak or untrue.
> Yet dearly I love you, and would be loved fain,
> But am betrothed unto your enemy;
> Divorce me, untie, or break that knot again,
> Take me to you, imprison me, for I,
> Except you enthrall me, never shall be free,
> Nor ever chaste, except you ravish me.
>
> (John Donne)

'IN NO STRANGE LAND'

'The Kingdom of God is within you'

O world invisible, we view thee,
O world intangible, we touch thee,
O world unknowable, we know thee,
Inapprehensible, we clutch thee!

Does the fish soar to find the ocean,
The eagle plunge to find the air—
That we ask of the stars in motion
If they have rumour of thee there?

Not where the wheeling systems darken,
And our benumbed conceiving soars!—
The drift of pinions, would we hearken,
Beats at our own clay-shuttered doors.

The angels keep their ancient places;—
Turn but a stone, and start a wing!
'Tis ye, 'tis your estrangèd faces,
That miss the many-splendoured thing.

But (when so sad thou canst not sadder)
Cry;—and upon thy so sore loss
Shall shine the traffic of Jacob's ladder
Pitched betwixt Heaven and Charing Cross.

Yea, in the night, my Soul, my daughter,
Cry,—clinging Heaven by the hems;
And lo, Christ walking on the water
Not of Genesareth, but Thames!

(Francis Thompson)

5.

AND as it is very easy to read too intellectually, so it is easier still to read too emotionally. Poetry which is a direct attack on the emotions is far more popular than any other kind of poetry, and the reason is not far to seek. What poetry does, as we have already said, is to co-ordinate responses, and the more superficial the response it asks for, the more easy it is to call it out. Common-place poems about home, love, nature, children, sorrow and silver linings are popular because all these things are the most familiar of stimuli, and there is a whole array of easy responses waiting on the threshold of our con-sciousness to respond at once to any of them. Now I do not mean at all that poems on these subjects are neces-sarily poor poems. I mean that it is easier to respond to poor poems on those subjects than to respond to good ones on the same subjects, because if all that is in a poem is already present on the surface of our consciousness, we naturally at once think it satisfying and satisfactory. It requires no fresh ordering of our minds, no reaching out of our faculties. It does not ask us to 'grow up'. To the lazy mind the perfect soul-mate is Echo.

But some practical examples will make the matter clearer, for by far the best way to train taste and to make discoveries in poetry is to compare one poem with another and so to feel with greater precision and scrupu-lousness exactly what is in each. I do not mean that we are to blame a poem for not being something which it never set out to be—to say that a little Elizabethan love song is not so good as Marvell's *To His Coy Mistress*, or that this epitaph by Wordsworth,

> These vales were saddened by a common gloom
> When good Jemima perished in her bloom,

is not so good as *Lycidas*. The success of a poem depends on what the poet is trying to do. But there is no better way of seeing what he has done, than by comparing it with a poem where some other poet is trying to do very much the same thing. Keats proved the truth of this about painting.

'A year ago I could not understand in the slightest degree Raphael's Cartoons—now I begin to read them a little. And how did I learn to do so? By seeing something done in quite an opposite spirit—I mean a picture of Guido's in which all the Saints, instead of that heroic simplicity and unaffected grandeur which they inherit from Raphael had each of them both in countenance and gesture all the canting, solemn, melodramatic mawkishness of Mackenzie's Father Nicholas.'

Compare, for example, Marvell's poem on a garden, quoted in the last chapter, with that popular piece of inanity, 'A garden is a lovesome thing, God wot!' The one all exquisite precision in thought, emotion and expression; the other pretentious, foolish and empty, appealing to nothing but the most shallow thinking and feeling. Or compare two poems on perhaps the most sentimental subject in the world—memories of mother-love in childhood. Eliza Cook's *The Old Armchair* was enormously popular in its own day, and is a very good example of a poem beloved entirely because of its subject matter. Nothing could be much lower than its technical level as verse, but it appealed to universal emotions, and is, indeed, as sincere as it is commonplace in its expression of those emotions.

> I love it, I love it; and who shall dare
> To chide me for loving that old arm-chair?
> I've treasured it long as a sainted prize;
> I've bedewed it with tears, and embalmed it with sighs.
> 'Tis bound by a thousand bands to my heart;
> Not a tie will break, not a link will start.
> Would ye learn the spell?—A mother sat there;
> And a sacred thing is that old arm-chair.
>
> In Childhood's hour I linger'd near
> The hallowed seat with listening ear;
> And gentle words that mother would give;
> To fit me to die, and teach me to live.

She told me shame would never betide
With truth for my creed and God for my guide;
She taught me to lisp my earliest prayer;
As I knelt beside that old arm-chair.

.   .   .   .   .   .

And now let us see the same sentiments operating at a much higher level of emotional sophistication and poetic achievement, in *Piano* by D. H. Lawrence.

Softly, in the dusk, a woman is singing to me;
Taking me back down the vista of years, till I see
A child sitting under the piano, in the boom of the tingling
    strings
And pressing the small, poised feet of a mother who smiles
    as she sings.

In spite of myself, the insidious mastery of song
Betrays me back, till the heart of me weeps to belong
To the old Sunday evenings at home, with winter outside
And hymns in the cosy parlour, the tinkling piano our guide.

So now it is vain for the singer to burst into clamour
With the great black piano appassionato. The glamour
Of childish days is upon me, my manhood is cast
Down in the flood of remembrance, I weep like a child for
    the past.

Here the sentimental theme is treated with no trace of sentimentality whatever. The emotion is neither false, nor vague, nor feeble, nor shallow, which are the things we mean by 'sentimental'. And see how much the poet has packed into those three short stanzas! The present and the past are both there, evoked in clear outline, and with equally clear-cut feeling. And all the simplicity of the child's world is there, and all the complexity and heartache of maturity—with the unique and particular twist of the individual poet in that subtle '*In spite of myself*, the *insidious* mastery of song *betrays* me back ...' which gives the whole 'tone' of the poem.

Eliza Cook's poem, in spite of the universality of its
theme, and its very genuine emotion, has no appeal in
the present day, because its manner and vocabulary is
that of a past generation, and there are no fashions
which go out of date quicker, and seem more ridiculous
when they are out of date, than fashions in minor poetry.
So a comparison is really more telling if we can find a
poem popular today which appeals at a low level of re-
sponse, and then compare it with something at a higher
level, which demands much more of the reader, and cor-
respondingly gives much more to him if he can enjoy it.
In *Cynara*, Ernest Dowson succeeds perfectly in creat-
ing a certain atmosphere of rather sordid and shabby
passion: what we might call the spirit of that recently
popular dance 'The Blues'. It is that very common mood
when, under the influence of dim or coloured lights,
swaying movement, monotonous and melodious rhythm,
and alcohol, the values of life appear to centre entirely
in the senses and the most superficial emotions, so that
the attitude of mind created in the poem takes on what
appears to be real significance and importance. So strong
is the spell and so skilful the versification, that it is quite
easy to mistake the sensuous excitement it creates, for
poetic excitement, though in a more detached critical
mood we may dismiss it as maudlin, hysterical gush.

CYNARA

Last night, ah, yesternight, betwixt her lips and mine
There fell thy shadow, Cynara! thy breath was shed
Upon my soul between the kisses and the wine;
And I was desolate and sick of an old passion,
    Yea, I was desolate and bow'd my head:
I have been faithful to thee, Cynara! in my fashion.

All night upon mine heart I felt her warm heart beat,
Night-long within mine arms in love and sleep she lay;

Surely the kisses of her bought red mouth were sweet;
But I was desolate and sick of an old passion,
   When I awoke and found the dawn was gray:
I have been faithful to thee, Cynara! in my fashion.

I have forgot much, Cynara! gone with the wind,
Flung roses, roses, riotously with the throng,
Dancing, to put thy pale lost lilies out of mind;
But I was desolate and sick of an old passion,
   Yea, all the time, because the dance was long:
I have been faithful to thee, Cynara! in my fashion.

I cried for madder music and for stronger wine,
But when the feast is finish'd and the lamps expire,
Then falls thy shadow, Cynara! the night is thine;
And I am desolate and sick of an old passion,
   Yea, hungry for the lips of my desire:
I have been faithful to thee, Cynara! in my fashion.

Now let us read a sixteenth century poem, by Sir
Thomas Wyatt on much the same theme: not a great
poem, perhaps, but a very much more distinguished one.

They flee from me, that sometime did me seek
   With naked foot, stalking in my chamber.
I have seen them gentle, tame and meek,
   That now are wild, and do not remember
   That sometime they put themselves in danger
      To take bread at my hand; and now they range
      Busily seeking with a continual change.

Thanked be fortune it hath been otherwise
   Twenty times better; but once, in special,
In thin array, after a pleasant guise,
   When her loose gown from her shoulders did fall,
   And she me caught in her arms long and small,
      Therewith all sweetly did me kiss
      And softly said, 'Dear heart how like you this?'

It was no dream; I lay broad waking:
  But all is turned, thorough my gentleness,
Into a strange fashion of forsaking;
  And I have leave to go of her goodness,
  And she also to use newfangleness.
    But since that I so kindly am served,
    I would fain know what she hath deserved.

It is not easy and obvious as *Cynara* is. It demands at once that the reader should adjust his faculties to a poetic experience—that is, an experience seized and presented in a special way of its own. In the first stanza it is presented in the form of symbol; in the second it is suggested and described; and in the third it is summed up and commented upon. At first sight the poem appears cold and formal beside *Cynara,* but with familiarity we see that this is because the poet has mastered and disciplined his emotion so that it exists independently of himself, as it were. The poet is outside the poem, its life is its own poetic life—the fusion of thought and feeling, of symbol and description and comment into a certain pattern of rhythmic language. *Cynara,* in spite of its melody, is formless. Its unity is in its monotony of tone and feeling, not in the just relationship of varied parts to a complete whole. While as far as the quality and flavour of the human emotion is concerned, Dowson differs as much from Wyatt as Guido from Raphael.

6.

JUST as we limit our responses if we read too intellectually or too emotionally, so too do we impoverish them if we cling too closely to the ideas of tradition, if we do not have enough sympathetic curiosity to welcome new ways with an open mind. 'All men,' says Wordsworth, 'feel an habitual gratitude, and something of an honorable bigotry, for the objects which have long continued to please them.' And again: 'It is supposed that by the act of writing in verse, an author makes a formal engagement that he will gratify certain known habits of association.' It is these two facts which have created the attitude of mind known as 'academic'. The word 'academic' is in disrepute: and with good reason. It implies the reader who is ruled in his decisions by convention. He shrinks from the shock of new experiments, he shelters behind the accepted, he bolsters himself up with authority, he will not plant himself on his own two feet, he is a slave to what Wordsworth calls 'that most dreadful enemy of our pleasures, our own pre-established codes of decision'. To approach reality from a new angle sends him scurrying back to the safe attitudes of the past, and he meets a new technique with a blank refusal even to try and understand it.

But one of the unconscious functions of poetry, and the chief conscious function of the interpreter of poetry, is to waken the dead. Not that those with any sort of appreciation of poetry are actually dead, but they are frequently in a state of perpetual hibernation. Mediocre poetry of all kinds is popular simply because people are willing to let their taste remain mediocre, that is all. The pleasure received from poor poetry implies a co-ordination it is true, but it is a very limited one. To illustrate again from physical control, we can compare it with the body at rest, or performing the average actions of daily life; walking, sitting, standing. We have only to see a fine athlete, or an acrobat, or a dancer, to have it brought home to us at once how much of the body's potentialities lie dormant in its daily use. And we have only to set out, however simply, to develop further physical suppleness, to realize the sense of pleasure and well-being which exercise inevitably brings. At once, something has come which was not there before: a sense of power has been added. To those who can master more

and more complex movements, more and more muscles
are involved and the harmony of their relationship be-
comes more and more intricate. Movement merges into
movement, and the supple tissues adapt themselves with
ever-increasing ease to whatever is demanded of them.

So it is with the tissues of the mind. They become
flabby with disuse, and the easy way of the familiar and
the commonplace is fatally attractive.

> Most souls, 'tis true, but peep out once an age,
> Dull sullen pris'ners in the body's cage:
> Dim lights of life, that burn a length of years,
> Useless, unseen, as lamps in sepulchres;
> Like Eastern kings a lazy state they keep,
> And close confined in their own palace, sleep.

To most people, reading poetry, if it is to mean any-
thing at all, is not easy. Why should it be? It is not the
things which are easy to come by which please longest
and please most. Poetry is the most concentrated and
complex use of language there is, and it is used as a
means of communication by men and women who live
more richly and intensely than we do. The result natu-
rally needs all that we can give of ourselves to meet it
and make it our own. I wish there were room here to
quote all the poems written by all the earnest Victorians
in praise of effort and application and perseverance and
patience and hope and faith! They might encourage the
readers of second-rate poetry to let themselves be swept
away from shallow, easy thinking and feeling, and on
to meet the challenge of fine poetry, the challenge of
clear feeling and clear thinking, of a wider and fuller
commerce with the whole of human consciousness, and
of the difficulty and the discipline and the delight of
words.

The mind of the skilled reader, like the muscles of
the trained athlete, adapts itself more and more easily

to the experiences of poetry. The new reader must inevitably win this plasticity from practice. But we must always remember poetry is to be read for delight. If after reading a poem several times as carefully and whole-heartedly as we can (aloud, for preference) it still does not 'suit the need of the moment', and we have no sense of flying to Parnassus, put it by and try something else. For, for every manner of person and for every shifting phase of personality, there is the poetry which satisfies. The endless adventure of reading it consists in marking in ourselves (and in others who share the adventure with us) the gradual waxing and waning of our capacities for 'organizing' our own vitality through that of the poet; in noting the gradual shiftings and changings of honest taste. In the appreciation of Ella Wheeler Wilcox lies the germ of the appreciation of Shakespeare. For that co-ordinating response to which poetry appeals —the sense of beauty—is organic: it is living. It has the principle of all life behind it, which means that it eternally changes and grows. It is a developing, expansive, fluid power, involving the personality not only in the clambering of stepping stones of our dead selves to higher things, but in the most varied discoveries of the realities of the human mind and heart and senses. Poems can come upon us in so many ways. Some knock us breathless with a triumphant sense of splendour; some steal soft-footed into the heart and curl themselves in the memory; some twine vinelike around our lives; some thrill us to action; some soothe us to rest; some lap us in the drowsy delight of dream; some have their necks clothed with thunder and some sing like the morning stars shouting for joy. Poetry is full of surprises. Some poems we outlive very quickly: some we grow to slowly: some step along life with us and are emotionally and intellectually inexhaustible like life itself. But as we read, every stage in our development seems the end, and we are prepared to justify our position of the moment with what seems to us insight and judgment. How soon—if we live fully and freely and read actively—have our responses unconsciously widened and deepened, so that it is the work of different poets which gives us satisfaction, and our enthusiasms of the past seem limited and lame.

Every true reader of poetry has experienced this sense of adventure, this gradual, unconscious increase and amplification of his capacities for poetic experience; this gradual refining and sensitizing and enlarging of his whole nature. And to any reader with the natural love of sharing discoveries with others, it is a sorry thought how many readers there are, who, through habit, through laziness, through rigidity of outlook, and perhaps most of all, simply through lack of training, have their potentialities standardized at a very low level, their responses atrophied, withered, stunted, so that their 'need of the moment' never reaches beyond the most mediocre poetry, and thus their heritage of stored vitality lies sterile.

COMMUNICATION VERSUS EXPRESSION

I.

DRYDEN declared that 'the first end of a writer is to be understood', and though that statement may demand a good deal of modification and expansion, it is tacitly accepted by the majority of what Dr. Johnson calls 'common readers' that it is the object of the poetic artist to communicate his experience to those who can see and hear his work: that his real aim, even if an unconscious one, is to interpret experience, as he had felt it, to his fellow men and women. I say, the aim may be an unconscious one, because I imagine that most poets, if taxed with having this aim in their writing, would strenuously deny that they worked with any idea of an audience in their consciousness. 'I feel assured I should write, for the mere yearning and fondness I have for the beautiful, even if my night's labours should be burnt every morning and no eye shine upon them,' wrote Keats, and perhaps every true poet would declare roundly that his concern was simply and solely to make the medium of words embody his experience in as intense and exact a form as was possible: to get the thing 'right'. It is generally found, however, that what the poet means by 'rightness', resolves itself into 'exactness of communication'; that he is unconsciously aiming either at some human norm of experience, or at an audience fit though few, and that the degree to which he has achieved giving expression to his own experience is a measure of the degree to which it arouses similar experience in those whom he unconsciously addresses.

But recently, this view that poetry is, basically, communication, has been directly challenged and flatly contradicted, and as a result, there is a body of modern poetry to a great deal of which the common reader finds himself quite unable to respond. Unwilling, somewhat naturally, to regard himself as feeble-minded, he prefers to think the poets have gone mad, and indeed a chance reading of a poem by any of the extremists is apt to encourage that view. It is, however, madness with a method in it, though sorting out the hawks from the handsaws is not an easy task.

Starting from the theory of Relativity, the group of poets who have been named 'modernist' points out that all human experience at any given moment is relative to the person who experiences it, and to the particular environment in which it takes place. It is, in fact, unique. It is made up of the relationship of a unique personality with unique circumstances in place and time. This isolation of every mood and moment, this inexorable procession of insecure and fleeting impressions, this shifting, indefinite interplay of elements and dimensions is human life. And the 'modernist' poet feels that a conception of life as anything so impermanent as this cannot possibly be suggested by any direct creative methods. He feels that there are no such things as the eternal and unchanging elements in human nature and human experience; that it is only individuals of blunted perceptions and reactions who can live or write by such empty generalizations; that it is impossible to present *his* consciousness of existence in the outworn terms of past approaches to existence, and that he must evolve an entirely new technique to express the unique character of his response.

Poetry, therefore, is a private affair of the poet. It is his business to find means of conveying, to himself, the unique quality of his experience in poetic form. He must surrender himself entirely to that experience and must seek until he find the selection and arrangement of words which shall, for him, evoke that particular experience in its entirety.

Up to this point, the position is not very different from that which every rebel from traditional methods has held. The poets did not wait for the theory of Relativity to be haunted by the impossibility of finding words for the unique quality of their individual experience, and new experiments and approaches have mated new blood with tradition in every age. But it is here that the 'modernist' parts company from the reader entirely. He must, he says, find the words which shall, for him, evoke his experience, but, he adds, it does not matter at all if the words have no meaning whatever for other people, or even if they have a completely different meaning. As Robert Graves tells us:

'In grammar the new poetic Relativity adopts the syntactical convention and thought level on which it is staged. This may be regular enough, but if the mood reaches a point in fantasia where grammar becomes frayed and snaps, then it can dispense with grammar.'

As far as language goes the modernist poet is precisely in the position of Humpty Dumpty.

"There's glory for you!"
"I don't know what you mean by 'glory'," Alice said.
Humpty Dumpty smiled contemptuously. "Of course you don't—till I tell you. I meant 'There's a nice knock-down argument for you!'"
"But 'glory' doesn't mean 'a nice knock-down argument'," Alice objected.

"When *I* use a word," Humpty Dumpty said, in rather a scornful tone, "it means just what I choose it to mean —neither more nor less."
"The question is," said Alice, "whether you *can* make words mean so many different things."
"The question is," said Humpty Dumpty, "which is to be master—that's all."

The poet is to be master—of his own experience and his expression of it—and that's all. His language is not the common tongue: it is *his* tongue. The extremists, indeed, seem determined to cut themselves off entirely from every tradition of poetic writing which civilization has evolved. It is almost as if they would go back to the conception of the poet as the magician who invented names for things. Gertrude Stein, the arch-modernist, sterilizes words in an aseptic method by which they are prevented from any of the associative contacts of the past, and freedom from all conventional bonds is the watchword of the whole school. Language must be absolutely free; there must be free association and dissociation of ideas and images, free versification, free syntax, free vocabulary, free spelling and free punctuation. In these conditions, the only thing which is incurably tightly shackled is—communication.

The result is this kind of poetry:

                    Among
                        these
                                    red pieces of
                    day (against which and
                    quite silently hills
                    made of blue and green paper

                    Scorchbend ingthem
                    -selves-U
                    pcurv E, into:

anguish (clim

b)ing
s-p-i-r-a
l
and, disappear)

Satanic and blasé

a black goat lookingly wanders

There is nothing left of the world but
into this noth
ing il treno per
Roma si-gnon ?
jerk
ilyr, ushes.

(E. E. Cummings)

To the exasperated comments of the logically minded
reader the modernist poet replies that he is not seeking
to communicate anything to the reader, or to withhold
anything from the reader; that his poem satisfies him and
expresses his private reaction to his private experience;
that it suggests the whole quality of that experience to
him, and that it is written and spelt and punctuated
in accordance with his own private catches of the breath
and pulse-rhythm and heart-beats. That he is, in fact,
talking aloud to himself in the poem, and that the reader
is overhearing him. He is not trying wilfully to be un-
intelligible to the reader, but he is not really concerned
with his reader at all. And he might quote J. S. Mill in
his defence: 'the peculiarity of poetry appears to us to
lie in the poet's utter unconsciousness of a listener.'
(Though here again there is an inclination to murmur
that the mere fact of publication almost seems to pre-
suppose a reader.)

This attitude of at one and the same time implying
the presence of a public, while deliberately ignoring it,
is, indeed, very difficult to understand, but the whole

question of this extremist view of what poetry is has been greatly clarified by Max Eastman in *The Literary Mind*, where the psychology of the situation is lucidly explained. Taking as his text that 'an artist is a man consecrated to the child's attitude toward values', Max Eastman illustrates, with quotations from the work of the child-psychologist Jean Piaget, the close parallel between the behaviour of the 'modernist' poet and of young children under eight years old.

'They seem to talk to each other a great deal ... but for the most part they are only talking to themselves. . . . Each one sticks to his own idea and is satisfied. . . He believes that someone is listening to him, and that is all he wants. He does not succeed in making his audience listen, because, as a matter of fact, he is not really addressing himself to it. He is talking aloud to himself in front of others. The audience is there simply as a stimulus. . . . The words have no social function.'

And again:

'The words spoken are not thought of from the point of view of the person spoken to. . . . Each child is shut up in his own point of view. . . . One of the facts which point most definitely to the ego-centric character of the explanations of children is the large proportion of cases in which the explainer completely forgets to name the objects which he is explaining.'

2.

THE parallel is certainly exact, and perhaps the type of poetry and its theories is best left with that comment and explanation. But to dismiss the creed that poetry is self-expression does not dismiss the difficulties of modern poetry, for the work of the poets who declare themselves to be quite sincerely aiming at communication is often as hard for the average reader to understand as the work of those who pretend to nothing but self-communion.

There is the poetry of T. S. Eliot, for example, deriving from the French 'Symbolists', whose difficulty depends mainly on his use of a private and personal imagery. He creates symbols which embody, for him, certain complex emotional experiences, and he uses these throughout his work as a kind of emotional shorthand. To himself, they convey a group of emotional relationships, just as a mathematical formula conveys a group of spatial relationships to a mathematician, but to the common reader they are incomprehensible until they are interpreted. We all possess these associative images in our experience: scenes or scents or colours which stand in our memories as symbols of emotional states, of other personalities, of places. Proust's whole marvellous prose epic of personality, *A la recherche du temps perdu*, is built up on the validity of such symbols. Or, to take a small illustration, there is a poem of Hardy in which he embodies the creation of such a one for him.

NEUTRAL TONES

We stood by a pond that winter day,
And the sun was white, as though chidden of God,
And a few leaves lay on the starving sod;
  —They had fallen from an ash, and were gray.

Your eyes on me were as eyes that rove
Over tedious riddles of years ago;
And some words played between us to and fro
  On which lost the more by our love.

The smile on your mouth was the deadest thing
Alive enough to have strength to die;
And a grin of bitterness swept thereby
  Like an ominous bird a-wing . . .

> Since then, keen lessons that love deceives,
> And wrings with wrong, have shaped to me
> Your face, and the God-curst sun, and a tree,
> And a pond edged with grayish leaves.

But if, in his poetry, whenever he wants to suggest that
love deceives, Hardy simply said 'the God-curst sun and
a tree and a pond edged with grayish leaves', his poems
would be very much more difficult to read than they are.

The Waste Land, and indeed all of Eliot's poetry, in
varying degrees, is built up of such personal symbols
and allusions, and until the significance and inter-
relationships of these have been made clear, the poems
remain unintelligible, and the symbols remain like meta-
phors detached from the subjects they illustrate, and de-
pending for their elucidation on the conjectural intuition
of the reader. 'To name an object,' says Mallarmé, the
founder of the French Symbolists, 'is to do away with
the three-quarters of the enjoyment of the poem which
is derived from the satisfaction of guessing little by lit-
tle: to suggest it, to evoke it, that is what charms the
imagination.' But the obvious weakness of this method
of writing and reading is that it is impossible for the
reader to know if he has guessed right, which is illus-
trated by the widely different, often completely con-
tradictory, comments on the same poem supplied by
rival critics.

Nor is it easy to take some of these critics very seri-
ously.

'The theme never appears in explicit statement. It is
formulated through a series of complex metaphors which
defy a paraphrasing of the sense into an equivalent prose.
The reader is plunged into a strangely unfamiliar milieu
of sensation, and the principle of its organization is not
immediately grasped. The logical meaning can never be
derived, but the poetical meaning is a direct intuition,

realized prior to an explicit knowledge of the subject matter of the poem. The poem does not convey: it presents.'

This comment by Allen Tate on the work of the American poet, Hart Crane, is typical of many. There is that reluctance to interpret, that insistence on plausible reasons for *not* interpreting, which cannot but rouse suspicions that the critic finds interpretation as difficult as the common reader. The common reader becomes even more suspicious when he finds that the poet himself, on being challenged to do so, has no difficulty at all in paraphrasing the sense into an equivalent prose.

The poem *At Melville's Tomb* (of which the first two verses are quoted below) was submitted to the American magazine *Poetry*.

> Often beneath the wave, wide from this ledge
> The dice of drowned men's bones he saw bequeath
> An embassy. Their numbers as he watched,
> Beat on the dusty shore and were obscured.
>
> And wrecks passed without sound of bells,
> The calyx of death's bounty giving back
> A scattered chapter, livid hieroglyph
> The portent wound in corridors of shells.

The editor, on receiving the poem, wrote to the author, and asked some pertinent questions: How *dice* can *bequeath an embassy*; and how a *calyx* can give back *a scattered chapter, livid hieroglyph*; and how, if it does, such a *portent* can be *wound in corridors?*

The author sent the following explanation:

'Dice bequeath an embassy, in the first place, by being ground (in this connection only, of course) in little cubes from the bones of drowned men by the action of the sea, and are finally thrown up on the sand having "numbers" but no identification. These being the bones of dead men who never completed their voyage, it seems legitimate to refer to them as the only surviving evidence of certain messages undelivered, mute evidence of certain things, experiences which the dead men might have had to deliver. . . .

This calyx refers in a double ironic sense both to a cornucopia and the vortex made by a sinking vessel. As soon as the water has closed over a ship this whirlpool sends up broken-spars, wreckage, etc., which can be alluded to as livid hieroglyphs making a scattered chapter so far as any complete record of the recent ship is concerned. In fact about as much definite knowledge might come from all this as anyone might gain from the roar of his own veins, which is easily heard by holding a shell close to one's ear.'

Once we have thus 'learnt the language', all is clear, and we are free to form an opinion on the way in which the poet has presented his experience, but until then we are in the position of Alice when she read *The Jabber-wocky*: 'somehow it seems to fill my head with ideas—only I don't know exactly what they are!' It is often enough clear, to a sensitive reader of modern poetry, from the poet's choice of words, from the texture of his language and the poise and movement of the actual syllables, that his work is a serious experiment which should be taken seriously. But this intuition that the lines *are* poetry, if he could but interpret them is of no more help to him in interpreting them than if they were in a foreign tongue. It is indeed an added exasperation; for no amount of rhythm and melody and word pattern can ever compensate for an ignorance of what the poet is talking about, and few poets are as accommodating in public interpretation as Hart Crane proved in this instance. They are usually more in the tone of Herbert Read: 'If you do not see, if you do not feel, you cannot understand.' Which reminds one of Ibsen's remark

'What I have said, I have said,' and of Bernard Shaw's comment: 'But the point is what he hasn't said he hasn't said.'

3.

In any attempt to analyze the problems of both poets and readers in the present day, there is always the initial problem of distinguishing between the true and the false originality. On the one hand the reader can say justly that he is willing to agree that experiment is the salt of art, but that he doesn't want to live on salt; and that those who never agree with public opinion are as much its slaves as those who never differ from it. There has been so much cocking of snoots at the bourgeoisie, so much self-conscious defiance of convention, so much bad-tempered scolding at tradition, so much ill-bred arrogance and intellectual snobbery, so many little 'movements' so soon out of date, so much humbug and so many pretensions in the field of modern poetry that a certain irritation on the part of the common reader is excusable.

On the other hand the sensitive reader knows that the public deserves most of the scorn the poets treat it with. 'I have not the slightest feeling of humility towards the public,' wrote Keats, 'a thing I cannot help looking upon as an enemy, and which I cannot address without feelings of hostility.' Fine poets do not write for the average reader, and never will. In every age the situation occurs which Wordsworth described in his preface to the *Lyrical Ballads*. 'Readers ... will frequently have to struggle with feelings of strangeness and awkwardness. They will look round for poetry, and will be induced to inquire by what species of courtesy these attempts can be permitted to assume that title.' In every age a new vision and a new technique have had to fight against the forces of convention and natural laziness of mind.

Always the old channels of communication have worn deep grooves and ruts in the minds of readers through which impressions slip swiftly and easily. To break a new track must take time and patience and goodwill. The spirit of one age changes to the spirit of the next almost imperceptibly. Gradually the evocative power of certain stimuli fade and are replaced by others. In one age ideas of immortality or the brotherhood of man win an easy hearing, in another ideas of the futility of existence and the isolation of the individual. Or the same subject will take on a completely different flavour according to the vocabulary of one century or another.

> Shall I, wasting in despair
> Die because a woman's fair?

becomes three hundred years later

> Shall I then hold the distaff firm,
> Nor hope to act discobolus,
> Leaving untried the outer spheres
> While woman slings the fatal shears?
> Shall I forgo my harmonies
> Clutching one waning stimulus?

The meaning of a new poet's words and rhythms is built up to the reader as they become familiar. The reader's response, stiff and clumsy at first, becomes gradually pliant and adaptable; a special 'sense' for a new poetry, analogous to the 'road sense' which develops from the driving of a car, grows as the new forms and language lose their strangeness. Nor is it till this sense has come that the poetry can be judged and its relation to the poetry of the past justly hazarded.

The poet of today has the same function as the poet of any other age, and strives towards the same end. Faced with all he has seen and heard and felt and thought and learnt of the universe and human life, he struggles to communicate his experience to his fellow men through the medium of language. And yet it is impossible for the reader of today to escape the conviction that his task of receiving the poet's communication is harder than that demanded of the readers of the past, and that nothing quite like the position in our present age has presented itself in the earlier history of poetry.

For one thing the older poets were kinder:

> "What is good fòr a bootless bene?"
>   With these dark words begins my Tale;
>   And their meaning is, whence can comfòrt spring
>   When prayer is of no avail?

It is all so thoughtful for the poor reader; but it is useless to have any hopes that we shall find the meanings of the dark words of the moderns translated so conveniently, and there are a great many dark words among them. But let us, nevertheless, make an attempt to analyze the reason for the feeling of bafflement which undoubtedly does assail the modern reader, however receptive to new influences he may try to be.

4.

THERE have always been 'difficult' poets. Shakespeare is the most difficult of all, and it is only because he appeals at so many different levels to so many different types of audience and reader that his difficulty has escaped much comment. There is so much else to say about him! But there are Donne and Blake and Gerard Manley Hopkins, all of whom demand the closest study to understand their meaning.

They illustrate two different types of obscurity in poetry which are quite distinct from each other. Blake is obscure—when he *is* obscure—because he will use words as arbitrarily as any 'modernist' poet does, to express meanings which are peculiar to himself alone. When Blake says:

> The caterpillar on the leaf
> Reminds thee of thy mother's grief,

it is merely nonsense to the common reader. There is nothing in his own experience to which he can possibly relate it. Blake, again, like T. S. Eliot, has a symbolic private language of his own which must be learnt before his longer poems can be read at all. But the difficulty of Shakespeare and Donne and Hopkins is quite different. It is the difficulty of abnormal compression and richness in the use of language, by which it is weighted with a supernormal significance. The words are packed with suggestion and overtones; there is not a syllable wasted and there may be omissions which the reader must supply for himself before he can achieve the full abundance of the poetic effect. Donne's *Nocturnal upon St. Lucy's Day*—that marvellous epitome of everything that is dead, cold, dark, and dreary—will illustrate what I mean:

> 'Tis the year's midnight, and it is the day's,
> Lucy's, who scarce seven hours herself unmasks;
>   The sun is spent, and now his flasks
>   Send forth light squibs, no constant rays;
>   The world's whole sap is sunk;
> The general balm th'hydroptic earth hath drunk,
> Whither, as to the bed's-feet, life is shrunk,
> Dead and interr'd; yet all these seem to laugh,
> Compared with me, who am their epitaph.
>
> Study me then, you who shall lovers be
> At the next world, that is, at the next spring;
>   For I am a very dead thing,
>   In whom Love wrought new alchemy.
>   For his art did express

A quintessence even from nothingness,
From dull privations, and lean emptiness;
He ruin'd me, and I am re-begot
Of absence, darkness, death; things which are not.

All others, from all things, draw all that's good,
Life, soul, form, spirit, whence they being have;
   I, by Love's limbec, am the grave
   Of all, that's nothing. Oft a flood
      Have we two wept, and so
Drown'd the whole world, us two; oft did we grow,
To be two chaoses, when we did show
Care to aught else; and often absences
Withdrew our souls, and made us carcasses.

But I am by her death—which word wrongs her—
Of the first nothing, the elixir grown;
   Were I a man, that I were one
   I needs must know; I should prefer,
      If I were any beast,
Some ends, some means; yea plants, yea stones detest,
And love; all, all some properties invest.
If I an ordinary nothing were,
As shadow, a light, and body must be here.

But I am none; nor will my sun renew.
You lovers, for whose sake, the lesser sun
   At this time to the Goat is run
   To fetch new lust, and give it you,
      Enjoy your summer all;
Since she enjoys her long night's festival,
Let me prepare towards her, and let me call
This hour her vigil, and her eve, since this
Both the year's and the day's deep midnight is.

Or this sonnet by Hopkins is an illustration of the same
type of concentration:

CARRION COMFORT

Not, I'll not, carrion comfort, Despair, not feast on thee;
Not untwist—slack they may be—these last strands of man
In me ór, most weary, cry I can no more. I can;
Can something, hope, wish day come, not choose not to be.
But ah, but O thou terrible, why wouldst thou rude on me
Thy wring-world right foot rock? lay a lionlimb against me?
    scan
With darksome devouring eyes my bruisèd bones? and fan,
O in turns of tempest, me heaped there; me frantic to avoid
    thee and flee?
Why? That my chaff might fly; my grain lie, sheer and clear.
Nay in all that toil, that coil, since (seems) I kissed the rod,
Hand rather, my heart lo! lapped strength, stole joy, would
    laugh, chéer.
Cheer whom though? the hero whose heaven-handling flung
    me, feet tród
Me? or me that fought him? O which one? Is it each one?
    That night, that year
Of now done darkness I wretch lay wrestling with (my God!)
    My God.

Real toughness of intellectual effort is needed to mas-
ter Hopkins, but once a 'Hopkins sense' has been devel-
oped by patience and practice, there is no poet whose
hold is stronger. None, too, who can illustrate better the
fact of how emotional acceptance can blot out com-
pletely all mere difference of creed.

5.

But the types of obscurity we have already mentioned,
though they are found in certain poets of the present
day, are not those which are peculiar to the moderns:
they are not peculiarly twentieth century obscurities. It
is often advanced by the defenders of the unintelligibil-
ity of modern poetry that all pioneers in poetic experi-

ment have been accused of obscurity, and that the outcry of the reader of poetry today is simply the natural rebellion of the conservative against the innovator, simply age crabbing youth as usual. But this is surely not so. There is no record that Donne was considered unintelligible in his own time, for example, and while Wordsworth was attacked as silly, Shelley as immoral and Keats as namby-pamby, they were not attacked as obscure. The only poet who has consistently had that charge brought against him is Blake, and he still remains obscure.

Is there then some special reason why the poetry written today should be hard to understand?

I think there is plenty of reason.

Poetry is a communication of experience, and the difficulty the poet of today finds in communicating his experience is first because the experience itself is actually different from that of the poets of the past. The human mind has enormously extended its self-consciousness, and this fact has revolutionized its outlook on existence. It is not merely that we all live in the machine age and that the poet finds himself in an environment which discusses psychology and Einstein, but it is that the attitude of sensitive man towards the place he holds in the universe has entirely changed.

Up to the end of the Victorian era, in spite of individual exceptions and the varieties in individual personalities, it can justly be said that man saw himself in the centre of a definitely mapped and defined scheme of absolute values. No great poet stands outside this scheme. Whatever the personal experience and the bent of mind and temperament which distinguishes him as an individual, this experience and temperament is enclosed within the outline of a faith. The faith may be explicit as in Browning or Wordsworth, or implicit, as in Chaucer or Shakespeare, but whether expressed or unexpressed, the stability of the poet's world and the validity of his experience are alike dependent on it.

The modern has no such scheme of absolute values. He has nothing but his own knowledge and emotion on which to build the foundations and the framework of his universe, and from which to fashion his faith. Ronald Bottrall speaks for many:

> all sap has gone out of tradition
> And the new limbs destined for full-leaved strewments
> Are withered, marrowless, natally thwarted.
>
> . . . we are dismembered,
> Into a myriad broken shadows,
> Each to himself reflected in a splinter of that glass
> Which we once knew as cosmos.

The identity of the self becomes the central fact of the universe, and the modern poet has naturally become conscious of that self with a degree of sensitiveness never before experienced. There are always the two great types of temperament, the types named by the psychologists extrovert and introvert—those who are mainly interested in looking out and those who are mainly interested in looking in, and there seems something in contemporary civilization which deflects those who look out from becoming poets. As a result, poetry tends more and more to be written by those to whom the conscious and unconscious workings of the individual human mind is the topic of supreme interest in life. What we may call the social element is completely lacking in the new poetry. And as the finest among this type of temperament inclines towards a highly developed intellectuality, the poets of distinction today are those whose experience is so specialized that it can only be communicated to a small, highly educated minority of their fellow men. It is therefore in poetry which the average reader finds it difficult, if not impossible, to grasp that the poet of today tells of his search for those values which he has himself painfully wrung from the impingement of his personal consciousness upon the facts of existence. Such poetry is Eliot's *Ash Wednesday,* or the following group of poems from contemporary writers.

REQUEST FOR OFFERING

Loose the baleful lion, snap
The frosty bars down from his cage
And unclasp the virgin pap
Of the white world to his rage.

See the innocent breast deny
But the bellowing shake down the air
Shudders of passion out of the sky
To shock, mangle and maim, tear.

Under the actual talons see
Virginal white and the black paw
Poised to slash on mystery
The five hates of a claw.

Amaze your eyes now, hard
Is the marble pap of the world
And the baleful lion regard
With the claws of paw curled.

Loose the baleful lion, snap
The frosty bars down from his cage
And unclasp the virgin pap
Of the white world to his rage.

(Richard Eberhart)

THE MAGNETIC MOUNTAIN

Somewhere beyond the railheads
Of reason, south or north,
Lies a magnetic mountain
Riveting sky to earth.

No line is laid so far.
Ties rusting in a stack
And sleepers—dead men's bones—
Mark a defeated track.

Kestrel who yearly changes
His tenement of space
At the last hovering
May signify that place.

Iron in the soul,
Spirit steeled in fire,
Needle trembling on truth—
These shall draw me there.

The planets hold their course,
Blindly the bee comes home,
And I shall need no sextant
To prove I'm getting warm.

Near that miraculous mountain
Compass and clock must fail,
For space stands on its head there
And time chases its tail.

There's iron for the asking
Will keep all winds at bay,
Girders to take the leaden
Strain of a sagging sky.

O there's a mine of metal,
Enough to make me rich
And build right over chaos
A cantilever bridge.

          (C. Day Lewis)

(from) THE LOOSENING

The Self:
  Not for nothing was I born
  Within earshot of that iron sea, where
  Across the hedge the calf milked
  Its mother astride the webbed dew and the share

Yearly uptore fresh paths beckoning the seed
To a resurrection. I have chopped logic
Since then and laid out the subject in
My brain's mortuary, held my mind
A clearing-house for moral commonplaces
Which gutter and are gone, yet I am sick
With excess of memory, how a farm-girl
Poised herself like a falcon at check
Amid the unfooted ploughland,
Laughter splashing from her mouth and
Rippling down her brown neck;
Not passion-rent she
But sensing in the bound
Of her breasts vigours to come, free
As air and powered to make her one
With the stream of earth-life around.

Unlearned, we hail with contumely or
Introverted joy the rain
Of irrigating dailiness, which leaves
The fields gleaming with hundred-fold grain.

(Ronald Bottrall)

We only have to compare these statements or sugges-
tions of faith with poems such as Donne's *Hymn to God
the Father,* Herbert's *The Pulley,* Clough's *Say not the
struggle nought availeth,* Tennyson's *In Memoriam,* to
realize how completely different is not only the actual
vocabulary, but the whole 'feel' of the poetry which
we think of as most characteristic of our own day, from
the traditional poetry which holds our hearts and habits.
So much grace and humanity seems lost; so much com-
fort and pity; so much music. There is a story told, I
think, by Robert Graves, of a governess who asked the
two little girls she taught, what the shape of the earth
was. Having been coached by a scientific elder brother
they replied glibly, 'It may conveniently be described
as an oblate spheroid'; to which the governess retorted,

'That may be so, and it may not be so, but it is certainly *nicer* for little girls to say that the earth is more or less the shape of an orange.' And it is very hard for the common reader not to feel that it is 'nicer' when the poets use the dear familiar words and forms of tradition!

As, however, we are faced with the inexorable fact of the new, we are better employed in seeking to understand its own aims and its own achievement, for the strangeness which we feel in its presence is more than the strangeness of a new view of experience. Indeed, when we examine them, the conclusions reached by the new poets have nothing new in them at all. The idea that submission and renunciation is the way of freedom (which is the theme of *Ash Wednesday*); the discoveries that identification with 'the stream of earth-life' in 'irrigating dailiness' brings harmony; that faith bridges chaos and that sacrifice and forgiveness breed peace, are no new faiths. But nevertheless the poetry in which they are here formulated is a new poetry.

It is new because the mental and emotional processes which have built it up are different from those of the past. The modern mind, as I have said, is acutely aware of itself and of its complex processes, and as a result the poet's use of his medium, of language, has become far more complex and self-conscious. Poetry has always relied on a super-logical use of language for its peculiar effects, but it has done so unconsciously, simply because it is natural for the poetic mind to work in that way. Nowadays many poets *deliberately* exclude the logical elements in thought from their poetry: they deliberately organize poetic thought as a *type* of thought distinct in itself from all other types of thought. They deliberately use language to convey thought *processes* rather than ideas: the quality and elements of thought, not the results of thought. They are intensely conscious of the fragmentary nature of all experience; of its dissociation: that man is at one and the same time a collection of cells, a system of electrons, an apparatus of reproduction, an instrument for good and evil, a nervous system, a bundle of habits, a machine, a spirit: that he may at one and the same time be suffering from the toothache, and be in love, and eat his dinner and blink his eyes, and be thinking about the Greek drama.

It is this type of experience which much modern poetry reflects, and which is at the root of its peculiar and elusive character. The poet who wishes it associates, without explanation, images or realities belonging to all these different facets of the conscious and the unconscious. He will juxtapose images and realities without distinguishing between them: he will ignore logical continuity to reflect the actual sequence of the dissociated impressions and perceptions from which his completed vision is fused.

Inevitably he demands from the reader a great deal more than the poet who is communicating a straightforward statement of emotion and idea. Unless the reader can attain to the same degree of perception as the poet; unless he has an intuitive understanding of the various phases of consciousness which are bridged and reconciled or contrasted in the poem, it remains for him an insoluble psychological puzzle. The weakness of this type of poetry as communication to the common reader is in just that fact, that the poet inevitably asks too much of the common reader, and that poetry, therefore, instead of being as of old, a common heritage, is inevitably becoming a very exclusive cult for very exclusive people.

FORM

I. ORGANIC RHYTHM

I.

LIFE is life and poetry is words. On the one side there is human experience, on the other certain symbols which we call language; and the technique of poetry is the way in which the poet chooses and arranges his symbols to communicate his experience. 'Poetry is the conversion of emotion into eloquence': it is the response the poet calls from words.

By words the poet masters his inspiration; bits it and bridles it and drives it to serve his artistic aim; by words he brings architecture to castles in the air; by words he makes us the inhabitants of a world which he alone can fashion; by words he creates Form.

Form is the outward symbol of that 'organization' which we have already analyzed as the function of poetry. Organization implies both order and vitality, and Form symbolizes therefore both order and vitality. What is generally meant by 'organizing ability' is very needful in poetry—orderliness, coherence, design—what Coleridge calls 'judgment ever awake and steady self-possession'. But the life of poetry is something beyond that. It is the perceiving of relationships in a certain peculiar way, and it is the manipulation and welding of significant words into the unique shape and pattern which shall communicate that perception.

The creative impulse is in itself formless—or nearly so. It is an excitement, an intoxication, a fire, a frenzy:

the completed poem is a work of art, a conscious com-
position, in which the poet strives to incarnate in mere
words the living glory of his inward vision. As Sir Wil-
liam Temple said: 'There must be a great agitation of
mind to invent, a great calm to judge and correct: there
must be upon the same tree and at the same time, both
flower and fruit.' The 'form' of the poem symbolizes the
unity of the inward vision, and it must create, control
and communicate everything which contributed to the
poet's experience—the frame of mind it occurred in, the
feelings it aroused, the suggestions which grew from it,
the conclusions it reached, its peculiar tone and colour
and flavour and atmosphere. And not only the actual
facts about all these, but the way in which they were
blended and balanced, harmonized and contrasted to
give them their individual and unique value. For it is
not perception by itself which makes poetry, but com-
pletely mastered and related perceptions: perfect unity
is the perfect relationship of parts to the whole. The
poem is this unity: it is the elucidation and fulfilment
of the creative impulse—it clarifies and intensifies the
experience by making it fully conscious, by giving it
complete detachment, by distilling its quality.

How the poet does this involves a discussion of all the
ways in which language can be used as an instrument to
interpret and relate thoughts, emotions and sensations:
it involves a discussion of rhythm and metre and rhyme
and imagery and ornament and words. We shall find no
help in rules. It is no use thinking of what Aristotle *said*,
we have got to find out what each poet *does*. And the
study of form in poetry begins when the reader's curi-
osity leads him, after he has felt the general effect of a
poem, to examine *how* this general effect is gained, and
to find the explanation of his feelings towards it in the
way in which the poet has woven his experience into the

warp and woof of language, into the structure and texture of words.

2.

THE first question with which the curious reader will challenge himself is the basic one of the difference between poetry and prose. What is the essential difference between experience presented in the form of poetry, and in the form of prose?

Now there is no doubt that the very sight of poetry on the page, before we have read a word of it, causes some effect on us. We instinctively prepare to give a certain special response, which we do not prepare for if we see a page of prose: we prepare to receive a certain special kind of experience. It is analogous to our feelings in a theatre. We prepare ourselves there also to give a special response and to receive a special kind of experience. We are to see and hear men and women act and speak, but to see and hear them with a difference. Their experience may arouse in us the same emotions as our own experience, but they are detached from any immediate relationship with us. They exist in a world of what is really artifice, a world of three-walled rooms and painted trees and make-up and electric light. The effect is to cut off the men and women on the stage from the practical affairs of our daily lives, and the effect of the sight of poetry is the same. It is to cut off the words on the page from the practical use we make of words in our daily lives, and more often than not this effect is immediately increased because, owing to the necessity for economy of language, the poet usually challenges the reader's attention by his opening words. He asks a question, *Why did I laugh tonight?*, or gives a cry, *So, so, break off this last lamenting kiss*, or makes an assertion, *Love, thou art absolute sole Lord of Life and Death*, or gives a command, *Go, lovely rose.* . . . And this use of words prepares us at once to receive a different experience from them.

The basis of this experience is *rhythm.*

Poetry, as we have already said, is ultimately a matter of the kind of vision which the poet creates, and not a matter of lines: it is ultimately a question of whether the poet takes the reader to a different level of consciousness. But this is no contradiction of the statement that its basis is rhythm. For that mood is created for the reader by the way in which the poet orders and organizes language—there is no other way in which the reader *can* partake of it, and it is only created by the presence of a sustained, unified, organic rhythm in language. This need not be verse rhythm, but it will inevitably be poetic rhythm: 'though the syllables may follow no apparent formula, the emotion will move along lines of power and order.'

It is perhaps wise to remind ourselves here that, from the point of view of appreciating poetry, rhythm, like beauty, is an experience in the reader. It becomes a question of whether the reader is a person who can only get the particular experience we call 'poetry' from an arrangement of words where some pattern of the time 'beat' is involved, or whether he is a person who can find poetic rhythm in an arrangement of words whose pattern does not contain that element of 'beat' at all. Not, of course, that with any reader the effects of rhythm cannot be limited to sound effects *only*. If they were, poetry in a foreign language would affect us as much as poetry in a familiar language. Sound and sense are inextricably blended in the total influence of the word pattern. It is only of recent years, however, that it has been accepted that rhythm can be entirely independent of any regularity of word stress whatever.

The earlier champions of free verse always declared that the sound rhythms of free verse were peculiar to itself and were as easily detectable from those of prose as from those of any regular verse pattern. This, however, is not so. Amy Lowell was invited to make experiments at Columbia University, and to read her own poems to the sphygmograph. The resulting records were indistinguishable from those of prose readings. This does not, of course, mean (as the enemies of free verse immediately declared) that free verse cannot be poetry. It merely means that we can obviously get the experiences we call 'poetry' from a use of language which, *judged purely as sound pattern,* is no different from prose. It means, in a word, that poetic rhythms need not be verse rhythms.

3.

WHAT, then, do we mean by poetic rhythm? The Greek word from which rhythm is derived means 'flow', and when we speak of poetic rhythm we mean the whole movement communicated by the words of the poem. Not only the sound movements, the pitch, stress and duration of the syllables, but the way in which the pattern of language directs and controls the ideas and feelings as well: the whole intellectual and emotional 'flow' of the poem.

Poetry, we have said, is ultimately an affair of the vision with which the poet 'apprehends', and the communication of that vision is the organic rhythm of the poem. The mood in which the vision is apprehended is the result of an abnormal discharge of nervous energy, of a raising of the level of consciousness at which the poet normally lives, of a fusing of faculties which normally operate independently, and it must by its very nature be transient. This is what Coleridge meant when he said that a long poem could not and should not be all poetry. He knew that for both poet and reader it was not possible to sustain the necessary intensity and concentration of effort for long. For it is with every poet as with Herrick.

> 'Tis not ev'ry day that I
> Fitted am to prophesy;
> No, but when the spirit fills
> The fantastic panicles,
> Full of fire, then I write
> As the Godhead doth indite.
> Thus enrag'd, my lines are hurl'd,
> Like the Sibyl's, through the world.
> Look how next the holy fire
> Either slakes or doth retire;
> So the fancy cools, till when
> That brave spirit comes again.

Organic or poetic rhythm, then, is obviously not a regular thing, like metre (regular sound pattern). It depends on the quality and duration of the inspiration of the poem. In a long dramatic or narrative poem there is the rhythm of the whole conception—the mood it is conceived in, and the shaping of its parts—and the alternations of rhythm within this outline to give variety of emotional tone and pitch. In a short poem, however, and we can only concern ourselves in this book with short poems, the poetic rhythm is a single unit. It is the realization of the experience in a certain mood: or as we have said earlier, the communication of the *quality* of the experience.

There is a very illuminating passage, in very bad verse, in a recently discovered notebook of Wordsworth, in which he describes the processes of unsuccessful and successful poetic creation. He tells how the creative passion drove him continually to

> burst forth
> In verse which, with a strong and random light
> Touching an object in its prominent parts,
> Created a memorial which to me
> Was all sufficient, and to my own mind
> Recalling the whole picture, seemed to speak
> An universal language. Scattering thus
> In passion many a desultory sound,
> I deemed that I had adequately clothed
> Meanings at which I hardly hinted, thought
> And forms of which I scarcely had produced
> An arbitrary sign—

And he goes on to state that this is not the 'poetic act', which lies

> In that considerate and laborious work,
> That patience which, admitting no neglect,
> By slow creation doth impart to speech
> Outline and substance even, till it has given
> A function kindred to organic power,
> The vital spirit of a perfect form.

It is that function kindred to organic power which is the soul and the secret of poetry. It is its presence or absence which create those distinctions between qualities of writing which so many critics have felt and have tried to define: the distinction between genius and talent, between imagination and fancy, between the literature of knowledge and the literature of power, between what is created and what is constructed. A dead body may have perfect symmetry of form, but it is not alive, and the same may be said of a great deal of poetry. When Herman Melville writes:

> No utter surprize can come to him
> Who reaches Shakespeare's core;
> That which we seek and shun is there—
> Man's final lore,

he expresses a profound truth, but it is not expressed in poetry. It is thought expressed in the form of poetry, but it is not 'poetic thought'. The poet has put an idea into verse, but the idea has come to him simply as an intellectual concept. It is not a fusion of various perceptions on different planes of experience—intellectual, emotional, sensuous. Again, when Coleridge writes

> Boys and girls,
> And women, that would groan to see a child
> Pull off an insect's leg, all read of war,
> The best amusement for our morning meal!

he makes an ironic comment in very blank verse. When A. E. Housman writes, in his *Epitaph on an Army of Mercenaries,*

> Their shoulders held the sky suspended;
>   They stood, and earth's foundations stay;
> What God abandoned, these defended,
>   And saved the sum of things for pay.

he creates a magnificent moment of ironic poetic thought. When Sir Ronald Ross had finally proved how the female mosquito transfers the infection of malaria, he put his sense of thrilling triumph into a poem, of which this is one verse.

> I know this little thing
>   A myriad men will save,
> O Death, where is thy sting,
>   Thy victory, O grave!

Whereas if we want to see how a great poet creates a sense of triumph we can read Donne's *The Anniversary.*

> All kings and all their favourites,
>   All glory of honours, beauties, wits,
> The sun itself, which makes times, as they pass,
> Is elder by a year, now, than it was
> When thou and I first one another saw:

All other things to their destruction draw,
    Only our love hath no decay;
This, no tomorrow hath, or yesterday,
Running it never runs from us away,
But truly keeps his first, last, everlasting day.

Even in this one verse (there are three in all), the central idea of the triumph of love is perceived and presented in relation to all earthly greatness and glory, to the sun itself, to death and decay, to time and eternity. And the central idea unifies and dominates them all.

4.

POETIC thought and purely logical thought differ completely in kind, and when they express themselves in poetic form we may call the one poetry and the other verse. But when we come to examine poetic thought more closely we find that within its own world there are numberless differences of degree, which determine the distinctions between good and mediocre and bad poetry.

As we have said before, subject matter has but little to do with the standards of value in poetry. A poem on a flea may be a very good poem and a poem on the immortality of the soul may be a very bad poem, and whether he is concerned about the utility or the futility of human life has no influence on the poet's technique. Hardy wrote some good pessimistic poems and Martin Tupper wrote some bad optimistic ones: Crabbe wrote some bad pessimistic ones and Browning wrote some good optimistic ones. The vitality of the poet's creation is the vitality he brings to the material, not the vitality of the material itself. It depends upon his power to fuse and present in words the varied elements which make up his poetic experience; to suggest or define the complex relationships which embody his vision. And it is the completeness and intensity and economy with which he does this which determines the poetic value of his poem.

The poet may have a splendid wealth of poetic vitality, but a lack of the very much less important, but still necessary 'organizing ability', to present it as he would. When Keats is criticizing his own *Endymion*, for instance, he declares very justly that he wrote it with genius but without 'judgment'. And later, when he is urging Shelley to be 'more of an artist', he says, 'Is not this extraordinary talk for the writer of *Endymion*, whose mind was like a pack of scattered cards? I am picked up and sorted to a pip. My imagination is a monastery and I am its monk.' It is that spirit of rigid discipline imposed upon the creative passion which stamps fine poetry. Coventry Patmore describes a great deal of lyric poetry as 'a kind of perception in a state of solution', which never becomes sufficiently concrete to be very serviceable or communicable, being mainly 'unintelligent heat'. This suggests very well a great body of poetry which, while it springs from a genuine poetic instinct and vision, misses that sense of finality which is the mark of the perfect work of art. D. H. Lawrence puts his finger on an example of it when he comments on Ralph Hodgson's *The Song of Honour*.

'It is the currency of poetry, not poetry itself. Every single line of it is poetic currency, but it isn't real poetry. It is exactly like a man who feels very strongly for a beggar and gives him a sovereign. . . . "Oh I do so want to give you this emotion," cries Hodgson. And so he takes out his poetic purse, and gives you a handful of cash and feels very strongly over it.'

The point is put most clearly, perhaps, by T. S. Eliot when he explains that the value of a poem depends on 'the intensity of the artistic process, the pressure, so to speak, under which the fusion takes place'. Has the poet waited until his material has become concentrated and welded into the organic verbal rhythm which is its complete consummation, or has expression come at a lower pressure, before unification is complete? Again a practical illustration of a success and a failure on the same theme will make the matter clearer. First one of Wordsworth's 'Lucy' poems:

> She dwelt among the untrodden ways
>   Beside the springs of Dove,
> A Maid whom there were none to praise
>   And very few to love:
>
> A violet by a mossy stone
>   Half hidden from the eye!
> Fair as a star, when only one
>   Is shining in the sky.
>
> She lived unknown, and few could know
>   When Lucy ceased to be;
> But she is in her grave, and oh,
>   The difference to me!

Now beside that put *Early Death* by Hartley Coleridge.

> She pass'd away like morning dew
>   Before the sun was high;
> So brief her time, she scarcely knew
>   The meaning of a sigh.
>
> As round the rose its soft perfume,
>   Sweet love around her floated;
> Admired she grew—while mortal doom
>   Crept on, unfear'd, unnoted.
>
> Love was her guardian Angel here,
>   But Love to Death resign'd her;
> Tho' love was kind, why should we fear
>   But holy Death is kinder.

The sense of perfect harmony which is created by the rhythm of the thought and feeling in *She dwelt among the untrodden ways* is all the stronger because it comes upon the reader unawares. The opening simplicity of the poem is deceptive. The direct flow of the first ten lines is so natural and quiet that we are unprepared for intensity. Then the impact of the final couplet, resolving all that has gone before into that shattering chord, and altering and enlarging suddenly the values of the whole by charging with emotional significance what had appeared to be a simple description, brings a sudden revelation, and lifts us at once into the world of pure poetry.

The second misses entirely this unity of effect, this sweep of inevitability, and moves altogether on a lower level of emotional co-ordination. There is a jolt in the flow at the opening of the second verse and its two last lines are really superfluous; while the change in the last verse from the concrete to the abstract, from the simple human figure, to the personification of Love and Death, distorts the original mood and blurs the outline. The pressure is too low.

5.

BUT quite apart from the degrees of completeness with which the poet achieves perfect organic rhythm in his creation, there are two great divisions or distinctions in the character of poetic rhythm, which are not distinctions in merit at all, but represent methods of presenting the theme—or perhaps are better described as two different modes or moods of poetic thought. There are exquisite poems written in both modes and any preference between the best of both is merely a personal one. These two great divisions are sometimes labelled Romantic and Classic, but as a fog of critical theory hangs about those definitions, it is perhaps simpler to speak of them as the personal and the impersonal methods of

presenting experience. An example will make the matter
clear. Take another of the 'Lucy' poems:

> A slumber did my spirit seal;
>   I had no human fears;
> She seemed a thing that could not feel
>   The touch of earthly years.
>
> No motion has she now, no force;
>   She neither hears nor sees;
> Rolled round in earth's diurnal course,
>   With rocks, and stones, and trees.

Now it is clear that this poem springs from a pro-
found personal emotion, and yet, when it is read, do we
think first of the emotion? I think not. First of all,
surely, we are at once conscious that it is a *poem*—that
it is a perfect piece of formal beauty, that in spite of
its deceptive appearance of artless simplicity, it is a
masterpiece of rhythmic organization. It is not until we
begin to examine it dispassionately as a piece of poetic
architecture that we have any idea of the concentration
of meaning which the words carry. The two verses are
not a mere sequence of thought and feeling; they inter-
lock with one another by the subtlest use of contrasted
suggestion. The slumber of the first verse—the seeming
death of sleep which numbs the poet's fears, balances
Lucy's sleep of death in the second. In the first she
seems untouchable by time, in the second she *is* untouch-
able by time: in the first we feel her vibrant, swift,
tingling with life, in the second she has no motion or
force or volition. And the use of the word 'thing' in the
first verse, having the meaning of a living spirit, with
the unspoken knowledge that she is only a dead 'thing'
in the second, is extraordinarily forcible.

The poem tells of a passionate human love and an
irreparable loss, but at the same time, it exists on an
entirely different level of consciousness from the actual

emotion of that love and loss. It is removed from it into a perfect serenity of rhythmical language, a language almost sculpturesque in its clear, clean economy of line.

Contrast it with the throb of the feeling, the actual catching of the sobbing breath, in a stanza of concentrated emotion presented in the personal mode, and written three hundred years before.

> O western wind, when will thou blow
> That the small rain down can rain?
> Christ, that my love were in my arms
> And I in my bed again!

In one, the concentration of impassioned reserve, in the other the concentration of direct intensity: in one the dramatic force of understatement, in the other the dramatic force of a cry of pain.

Or let us take two more examples of the same theme as the Lucy poem—the theme of love and loss—presented in two other poetic rhythms, both impersonal, but with the impersonality of two personalities quite different from each other and different again from Wordsworth.

THE TWA CORBIES

> As I was walking all alane
> I heard twa corbies making a mane:
> The ane unto the tither did say,
> 'Whar sall we gang and dine the day?'
>
> '—In behint yon auld fail dyke
> I wot there lies a new-slain knight;
> And naebody kens that he lies there
> But his hawk, his hound and his lady fair.
>
> 'His hound is to the hunting gane
> His hawk to fetch the wild-fowl hame,
> His lady's ta'en anither mate,
> So we may mak our dinner sweet.

'Ye'll sit on his white hause-bane
And I'll pike out his bonny blue e'en:
Wi' ae lock o' his gowden hair
We'll theek our nest when it grows bare.

'Mony a one for him maks mane,
But nane sall ken whar he is gane:
O'er his white banes, when they are bare,
The wind sall blaw for evermair.'

In this old ballad the impersonality is that of the dramatist. The reader, instead of being spoken to directly, overhears the conversation of the characters in the poem. And this conversation tells a story, and presents a situation, and etches a series of pictures, and creates an atmosphere. There is material for a five act tragedy compressed into the five four-lined verses, and it is completely impersonal. We have no sense at all of the poet except as the creator of the poem.

In *The Song of the Mad Prince*, by Walter de la Mare, the dramatic method and oblique approach, the building up of the unity of the organic rhythm by hints and flashes, by suppressions and surprises, is pushed still further. It is a poem which proves how possible it is to know literally almost nothing about the prose 'meaning' of a poem while giving it instant recognition as poetry. No paraphrase could 'explain' it. Its effect is gained out of the most elusive, unsubstantial materials, by suggestion and implication, by half-statements and half-resolved nonsense, and yet as a piece of poetic form it stands four-square, impregnable, complete. There is something of the atmosphere of Wordsworth in it and something of the old ballads, but it is itself alone. It is indeed a very good example of the unmistakable 'signature' which belongs to the true poet however impersonal his mood. It might be possible to mistake the first verse, but the flow of the last six lines, the atmosphere woven of eve's loveliness and green dusk, and dreams and life's troubled bubble, and the elusive dramatic central figure could be the creation of no other writer.

> Who said 'Peacock Pie'?
>   The old King to the sparrow:
> Who said, 'Crops are ripe'?
>   Rust to the harrow:
> Who said, 'Where sleeps she now?
>   Where rests she now her head,
> Bathed in eve's loveliness?'
>   That's what I said.
>
> Who said, 'Ay, mum's the word'?
>   Sexton to willow:
> Who said, 'Green dusk for dreams,
>   Moss for a pillow'?
> Who said, 'All Time's delight
>   Hath she for narrow bed;
> Life's troubled bubble broken'?
>   That's what I said.

In contrast again to these two, take a sonnet by another poet with an unmistakable signature, W. B. Yeats, where personal emotion throbs in every line, and we are saturated in it, carried along with it, feeling its ebb and flow continuously in our own blood and nerves.

THE FOLLY OF BEING COMFORTED

> One that is ever kind said yesterday:
> "Your well-beloved's hair has threads of grey,
> And little shadows come about her eyes;
> Time can but make it easier to be wise
> Though now it seem impossible, and so
> Patience is all that you have need of."
>   No,
>
> I have not a crumb of comfort, not a grain,
> Time can but make her beauty over again:

Because of that great nobleness of hers
The fire that stirs about her, when she stirs
Burns but more clearly. O she had not these ways,
When all the wild summer was in her gaze.
O heart! O heart! if she'd but turn her head,
You'd know the folly of being comforted.

At once we feel ourselves in the other great poetic mood. It would be quite idle to compare this with the 'Lucy' poem as to merit: both poems are masterpieces, but at once we sense a difference in the way the emotion is handled. Wordsworth is *outside* the poem: Yeats is *inside* it, and so are we as we read it. We are identified with his direct emotion. As soon as we have learnt, in the first six lines, what the theme is, we partake of all the turmoil and pain and rebellion which have shaken the poet's heart at the thought of the passing of beauty. We do not think first of the formal perfection, we think of little but that complex passion in the poet's heart. For the total emotional effect here is not a simple one as in O *western wind, when will thou blow?* It is compact of faith and at the same time a trembling, half-strangled fear; that simultaneous doubt and longing for assurance which forces him to say 'I have not a crumb of comfort' in place of 'I need not a crumb...' and which later makes him interrupt his proud song of her inextinguishable grace and dignity, by the passionate craving for some sign which shall create in him an immediate sense of security. Nor is the emotion a purely personal one, related only to the characters in the poem. There is an undercurrent of something far more, a blending of the actual and the abstract, the universal and the particular, the whole heartache of the world at the inexorable coming of age, as well as the personal passion of revolt of the poet himself at the change in his beloved.

But at the end we have no sense of serenity. It is with

the heart fluttering and the mind questioning that we go back to analyze the technical means by which this effect has been caused in us. And this is the outstanding difference between the rhythms of classical and romantic poetry. Impersonal rhythms seem always to come back to where they started from—full circle. *They are absolutely enclosed within the framework of the poem.* Personal rhythms seem to throb on in the air: they overflow the boundaries of the verse and refuse to be enclosed within the formal framework, however beautiful. They never seem to have become detached from the living heart of the poet's personality and to have completely independent life.

To conclude this section we will take a poem by Hopkins on the same theme as the Yeats sonnet, but treated in the impersonal mood.

> Márgarét, are you gríeving
> Over Goldengrove unleaving?
> Leáves, like the things of man, you
> With your fresh thoughts care for, can
>   you?
> Áh, ás the heart grows older
> It will come to such sights colder
> By and by, nor spare a sigh
> Though worlds of wanwood leafmeal lie;
> And yet you will weep and know why.
> Now no matter, child, the name:
> Sórrow's spríngs áre the same.
> Nor mouth had, no nor mind, expressed
> What heart heard of, ghost guessed:
> It ís the blight man was born for,
> It is Margaret you mourn for.

At first sight it seems cold, curt and hard beside the pulsing, breathing fire of Yeats's passion, but there is matter for a lifetime of thought and feeling compressed into the few short lines. So concentrated indeed is the communication, that the words can barely carry the weight he loads them with: he laces his sense so tightly that it can hardly breathe. To unravel the thread of the argument it must be stretched to twice its length and even then some lines remain ambiguous. But the structure of the intellectual and emotional movement is a complete unity. The question with which it opens,

> Margaret, are you grieving
> Over Goldengrove unleaving?

develops to its inevitable and profound solution in the final couplet—this grief over the inexorable hand of Time as felt by the child in the fall of the leaves in her favourite wood, is the central grief of the whole human race.

> It is the blight man was born for,
> It is Margaret you mourn for.

Again it would be futile to say one of these poems was 'better' than the other. Each is a supreme achievement in its own rhythm.

6.

THE most characteristic poet of the present day, T. S. Eliot, has created rhythms in the language which are entirely original and his own, and since his poetry is difficult poetry for the common reader, and since an understanding of the way in which he 'organizes' his experience is essential to a comprehension of his poetry, it is worth while to attempt some analysis of his methods. Their originality will be seen at its most startling if we compare his treatment of a theme with the treatment of the same theme by a typical Victorian. It is that of disillusionment, of the discovery of the contrast between

dream and reality which inevitably awaits the sensitive
liver of life.

.   .   .   .   .   .

The sea of faith
Was once, too, at the full, and round earth's shore
Lay like the folds of a bright girdle furl'd;
But now I only hear
Its melancholy, long, withdrawing roar,
Retreating to the breath
Of the night-wind down the vast edges drear
And naked shingles of the world.

.   .   .   .   .   .

A COOKING EGG

En l'an trentiesme de mon aage
Que toutes mes hontes j'ay beues...

Pipit sate upright in her chair
    Some distance from where I was sitting;
Views of the Oxford Colleges
    Lay on the table, with the knitting.

Daguerreotypes and silhouettes,
    Her grandfather and great great aunts,
Supported on the mantelpiece
    An *Invitation to the Dance.*

.   .   .   .   .   .

I shall not want Honour in Heaven
    For I shall meet Sir Philip Sidney
And have talk with Coriolanus
    And other heroes of that kidney.

I shall not want Capital in Heaven
    For I shall meet Sir Alfred Mond:
We two shall lie together, lapt
    In a five per cent. Exchequer Bond.

I shall not want Society in Heaven
     Lucretia Borgia shall be my Bride;
Her anecdotes will be more amusing
     Than Pipit's experience could provide.

I shall not want Pipit in Heaven:
     Madame Blavatsky will instruct me
In the Seven Sacred Trances;
     Piccarda de Donati will conduct me . . .

·   ·   ·   ·   ·   ∫

But where is the penny world I bought
     To eat with Pipit behind the screen?
The red-eyed scavengers are creeping
     From Kentish Town and Golder's Green;

Where are the eagles and the trumpets?

     Buried beneath some snow-deep Alps.
Over buttered scones and crumpets
     Weeping, weeping multitudes
Droop in a hundred A.B.C.'s.

Eliot is saying the same thing as Matthew Arnold, but
it would be difficult to find two more different methods
of setting about saying it, two more different moods or
modes of poetic rhythm. The one proceeds by a logical
series of statements: the other by a series of discrete,
apparently unrelated observations with no narrative or
intellectual sequence.

First of all what are these fragments which coalesce
to form the poem?

The poet, at the age of thirty, and Pipit, who is pre-
sumably his old nurse, are sitting together in her room.
It is the typical room of her kind: the *Views of the Ox-
ford Colleges* which he has given her when he was at the
university, are on the table, the typical pictures are on
the wall. As he sits there he remembers the days when he
was a child in the same room, when he would buy penny

oranges to eat with Pipit, and think of them as the world which was to be his oyster, and of the life of a grown man, which was going to be like Heaven, and in which he saw himself as the most romantic, wealthy, distinguished and exceptional of figures. Where have all these visions gone? They are buried far far out of sight. The realities of the world can be symbolized by the rat-like swarms which haunt the London suburbs, and the dreary multitudes who eat in cheap tea-shops.

It is clear that the poetic rhythm in *A Cooking Egg* is something quite different from anything we have yet examined. The poem has an intellectual and emotional 'flow', but it is not the same sort of intellectual and emotional flow as in any of the other poems we have quoted, nor is it communicated in the same way. We have already discussed the new consciousness of the com-position of human experience which moulds the poetic mood of many of the moderns: the new concern with the direct processes and workings of the human nervous system. It is this which conditions all the poetry of T. S. Eliot. All the methods used by former poets to present and develop their themes depend on the resolution of logical relationships and sequences of emotional and in-tellectual experience. Eliot's quite deliberately does not. He would, I imagine, associate himself with the words of the American poet, Hart Crane, in his comment on his own similar ideals of poetic form.

'... If the poet is to be held completely to the already evolved and exploited sequences of imagery and logic, what field of added consciousness and increased percep-tion ... can be expected when one has to relatively re-turn to the alphabet every breath or so? In the minds of people who have sensitively read, seen and experienced a great deal, isn't there a terminology something like shorthand as compared to usual description and dialec-tics, which the artist ought to be right in trusting as a reasonable connective agent toward fresh concepts, more inclusive valuations?'

It is on the assumption that there is such a shorthand that T. S. Eliot writes. *A Cooking Egg* is a simple illustration of what can become a far more complex matter. The reader has to fill in some gaps and deduce changes of time and place and mood without these being specified, but there are really only two strands in the pattern, two pieces to the puzzle, representing the past and the present, and they join neatly and symmetrically, like the elementary square blocks with which children make pictures in the nursery. But Eliot's formal architecture can be more like the assembling of a very complicated and difficult jigsaw. Nor, perhaps, is that image a just one— no image of inorganic growth and being is a just image for poetry (unless it be bad poetry). It is better perhaps to speak in direct language and to say that the unity of *The Waste Land* is the unity not of an idea but of a total human consciousness: it is not a unity in the sense that a logical argument or a well built plot is a unity, with a beginning, a middle and an end, it is unified in the sense that a personality is a unity. Its organic system is a relationship of different planes of experience to each other in a very complex way; a fusing of observation, sensation, memory, learning, fact; of the physical and emotional and intellectual and moral; of the past and the present, the realistic and the symbolic, the direct and the suggestive; of statement and memory, perception and reflexion, profundity and froth. We have said that this fusing of different planes of experience is of the very essence of all poetry, and that is true. But Eliot's poetic method differs from that of earlier poets in his deliberate ignoring of *logical* association of experience. His poetic symbolism is incoherent with the incoherence of unconscious mental association, and swift with the swift nimbleness of thought. The characters and background, as well as the direction and quality of the structure, change continually and without warning, while the vocabulary leaps from that of the scholar to that of the scullion, from the heights of romance to the dregs of realism as the moods and rhythms shift and change.

For a practical illustration of it, I will quote parts of the second section of *The Waste Land*, called 'A Game of Chess'. The title refers to a game of chess in a play by Middleton, *Women beware Women*, presumably also to the stage direction of Ferdinand and Miranda playing chess in *The Tempest*. The theme is sexual love.

> The Chair she sat in, like a burnished throne,
> Glowed on the marble, where the glass
> Held up by standards wrought with fruited vines
> From which a golden Cupidon peeped out
> (Another hid his eyes behind his wing)
> Doubled the flames of sevenbranched candelabra
> Reflecting light upon the table as
> The glitter of her jewels rose to meet it,
> From satin cases poured in rich profusion;
> In vials of ivory and coloured glass
> Unstoppered, lurked her strange synthetic perfumes,
> Unguent, powdered, or liquid—troubled, confused
> And drowned the sense in odours; . . .
>
> Above the antique mantel was displayed
> As though a window gave upon the sylvan scene
> The change of Philomel, by the barbarous king
> So rudely forced; yet there the nightingale
> Filled all the desert with inviolable voice
> And still she cried, and still the world pursues,
> "Jug Jug" to dirty ears.
> And other withered stumps of time
> Were told upon the walls; staring forms
> Leaned out, leaning, hushing the room enclosed.

Footsteps shuffled on the stair.
Under the firelight, under the brush, her hair
Spread out in fiery points
Glowed into words, then would be savagely still.

"My nerves are bad to-night. Yes, bad. Stay with me.
"Speak to me. Why do you never speak. Speak.
"What are you thinking of? What thinking?
       What?
"I never know what you are thinking. Think."

I think we are in rats' alley
Where the dead men lost their bones.

"What is that noise?"
                    The wind under the door.
"What is that noise now? What is the wind doing?"
                    Nothing again nothing.
                              "Do
"You know nothing? Do you see nothing? Do you
    remember
"Nothing?"
           I remember
Those are pearls that were his eyes.
"Are you alive, or not? Is there nothing in your head?"
                                        But

O O O O that Shakespeherian Rag—
It's so elegant
So intelligent
"What shall I do now? What shall I do?"
"I shall rush out as I am, and walk the street
"With my hair down, so. What shall we do to-morrow?
"What shall we ever do?"

                         The hot water at ten.
And if it rains, a closed car at four.
And we shall play a game of chess,
Pressing lidless eyes and waiting for a knock upon
    the door.

When Lil's husband got demobbed, I said—
I didn't mince my words, I said to her myself,
HURRY UP PLEASE ITS TIME
Now Albert's coming back, make yourself a bit
    smart. . . .

He's been in the army four years, he wants a good
    time,
And if you don't give it him, there's others will, I said.
Oh is there, she said. Something o' that, I said.
Then I'll know who to thank, she said, and give me a
    straight look.
HURRY UP PLEASE ITS TIME
If you don't like it you can get on with it, I said. . . .

You ought to be ashamed, I said, to look so antique.
(And her only thirty-one)
I can't help it, she said, pulling a long face,
It's them pills I took, to bring it off, she said.
(She's had five already, and nearly died of young
    George.)
The chemist said it would be all right, but I've never
    been the same.
You *are* a proper fool, I said.
Well, if Albert won't leave you alone, there it is, I
    said,
What you get married for if you don't want children?
HURRY UP PLEASE ITS TIME
Well that Sunday Albert was home, they had a hot
    gammon,
And they asked me to dinner, to get the beauty of
    it hot.
HURRY UP PLEASE ITS TIME
HURRY UP PLEASE ITS TIME
Goonight Bill. Goonight Lou. Goonight May.
    Goonight.
Ta ta. Goonight. Goonight.
Good night, ladies, good night, sweet ladies, good
    night, good night.

I will attempt a rough analysis of what I believe the poet is presenting, and how by his individual use of symbol, of image, of suggestion, of verbal rhythm, of tone, of vocabulary, he presents it.

We are at once in the atmosphere of the glories of romantic passion. The memory of Cleopatra on her barge introduces a similar scene of imagined richness and exuberance. Yet even here we are reminded of what love may be, by a picture over the mantel of the story of the rape of Philomela as described by Ovid. A horrible tale of lust and barbarism, but, in the form of a nightingale, Philomela kept her voice inviolate, and beautified the desert. Now, the world is still as cruel as Tereus and the nightingale still sings to barbarians.

Without explanation, the background changes to a personal memory of a scene between the poet and a woman. Rigid in his sterile emotional restraint, he is quite incapable of bringing her happiness or comfort. Their relationship has no freedom or joy or natural human feeling. His imagination is haunted by thoughts of death: he is dying of thirst in sight of water. His mind can remember the sea-song in *The Tempest,* while emotionally he remains entirely negative and inhibited.

Then the shrill syncopation of jazz and all the sophistication and emptiness of modern society blot out Shakespeare. Hysteria and the artificialities of social appearances are all that the relationships of the sexes mean to these people.

Again the poet uses his seven league boots and the environment changes. Is love any more real and free among the lower classes? The refrain 'Hurry up please its time' marks the scene as a 'pub' at the closing hour. One woman is giving her opinions of life and love to another, and incidentally a revelation of all the standards and values by which she and her like live. Finally she and her friends leave, the 'pub' closes its doors, and all the difference between its world, and the neurotic, artificial world, and the sane, rich, Shakespearean world is in the irony of the last line. The words are almost the same, while the whole emotional, moral, intellectual and physical atmosphere evoked by them are on an entirely different plane of experience.

Once the sequence of idea and feeling has been grasped here, it is impossible not to admire the technical brilliance of the 'ordering' of the material. To turn fresh from a reading of some masterpiece of technical control in the traditional manner—Keats's *Ode to a Nightingale* or Meredith's *The Woods of Westermain*, for example, is at first to have the sensation of turning from listening to a Mozart sonata, to a prolonged tuning up of an orchestra with nothing to follow. But once the 'Eliot sense' is somewhat developed, the pattern can soon be detected, and is seen and felt to be the creation of an original and provocative poetic rhythm, by an original and provocative personality. It has not the emotional richness and vitality of the great artist, but it is a most vivid presentation of an intense, if narrow, personal vision. The plight of a man of exceptional nervous and intellectual sensitiveness in the modern world; his sense of its worthlessness and sordidness and ugliness, and of his own emotional inadequacy to it; with the contrasts between it and all that his mature intellectual and artistic consciousness holds, could hardly be projected more forcibly than in Eliot's early poems and *The Waste Land*. In *Ash Wednesday*, there is a change, and though it is even more unintelligible to the common reader than the earlier work, there is a subtle shifting of the whole rhythmic structure. Emotional affirmation and assurance seem to replace the neurotic and tortured restlessness of *The Waste Land*. Mr. Eliot has stated that genuine po-

etry can communicate before it is understood, and there
is no doubt that even without an intellectual grasp of
the prose 'meaning' of the poem, the sensitive reader
feels that he is in the presence of something which is
undoubtedly poetry of a high order. But this is not
enough to base a judgment upon, and there must be
very few readers who can combine the necessary appre-
hension *and* comprehension to interpret fully the or-
ganic rhythms of the whole.

II. PROSODY AND SOUND PATTERN

I.

THE technique of poetry deals with the various ways
by which the poet communicates to the reader what we
have called the organic rhythm of his experience. His
'poetic thought' moulds itself into a certain flow or
pattern of words. It is not moulded in the sense in which
a cook pours cornflour blancmange into a shape—ob-
long, circular, battlemented, or crowned with the like-
ness of a pineapple *couchant*: poetic form does not
demand regularity or symmetry or any kind of fixed
proportion, though it may have it. The poet fits the
pattern to the material, not the material to the pattern.
He may create an entirely fresh rhythm, or he may
adapt an old form: he may demand complete freedom
of metrical arrangement or he may impose on himself
the most rigid rules. But his aim is always to find the
verbal rhythm which shall be the nearest equivalent he
can get to the organic rhythm of his 'inspiration'. His
poem may be ruined by a clumsy adjustment of matter
and manner. Cowper, for example, ruined his *Verses
supposed to be written by Alexander Selkirk* by a wrong
choice of form.

> I am monarch of all I survey
>   My right there is none to dispute;
> From the centre all round to the sea,
>   I am lord of the fowl and the brute.
> Oh, Solitude! where are thy charms
>   That sages have seen in thy face?
> Better dwell in the midst of alarms,
>   Than reign in this horrible place

—a sound pattern more suited to comic opera than to expressing the horrors of solitude. Or another example of how an effect can be spoilt by an inattention to design, is the common printing of extracts from Donne's *The Extasie* as if it were a short poem in four-lined stanzas. It is as a matter of fact a poem of more than seventy continuous lines, and a very real and important part of its emotional effect is in its continuity and uninterrupted flow, which carries along its impassioned apprehension of the relation of the soul to the body, in one uninterrupted sweep of poetic flight.

But though certain metrical arrangements may seem specially favorable or unfavorable to certain types of material, it is quite possible for different poets to use the same abstract form to convey completely opposite effects, so that the reader can hardly believe that a handbook of prosody would class the metres as the same. Keats's *Lamia,* for instance, is in the same form as Pope's *Rape of the Lock,* and Crashaw's *Hymn to St. Teresa* as Marvell's *To his Coy Mistress.* It is, perhaps, worth quoting a passage from each of these in illustration of the point, for as the poets are contemporaries it is stranger still that such utterly different emotional rhythms should be evoked by the same basic sound pattern.

> Love, thou art Absolute sole lord
> Of Life and Death. To prove the word,

We'll now appeal to none of all
Those thy old Soldiers, Great and tall,
Ripe Men of Martyrdom, that could reach down
With strong arms, their triumphant crown;
Such as could with lusty breath
Speak loud into the face of death
Their Great Lord's glorious name, to none
Of those whose spacious Bosoms spread a throne
For Love at large to fill; spare blood and
      sweat,
And see him take a private seat,
Making his mansion in the mild
And milky soul of a soft child.

*

Now therefore, while the youthful hue
Sits on thy skin like morning dew
And while thy willing Soul transpires
At every pore with instant Fires,
Now let us sport us while we may;
And now, like am'rous birds of prey,
Rather at once our Time devour,
Than languish in his slow-chapt pow'r.
Let us roll all our Strength, and all
Our sweetness, up into one Ball:
And tear our Pleasures with rough strife,
Thorough the iron gates of Life.
Thus, though we cannot make our Sun
Stand still, yet we will make him run.

2.

To attempt to reduce poetry to rules, to make laws of
prosody into a body of policemen to keep poetry in
order, is, indeed, quite futile. D. H. Lawrence is right
when he declares that the measurement of lines by feet
and stress, with its suggestion of footsteps hitting the
earth, is all wrong.

'I think more of a bird with broad wings flying and lapsing through the air, than anything, when I think of metre. . . . It all depends on the *pause*—the natural pause, the natural lingering of the voice according to the feeling—it is the hidden emotional pattern that makes poetry, not the obvious form. It doesn't depend on ear, particularly, but on the sensitive soul. And the ear gets a habit and becomes master, when the ebbing and lifting emotion should be master, and the ear the transmitter. If your ear has got stiff and a bit mechanical, don't blame my poetry.'

It is the claim that the hidden emotional pattern makes the poem and not the outward form, which is behind the whole free verse movement—the idea that the modulations of individual and therefore unique thought and feeling must find an exact counterpart in some unique modulation of rhythm and cadence. It is true that successful poems where the structure simply follows the rhythms of the emotion can be extraordinarily lovely and satisfying.

PHILOMELA

Hark! ah, the nightingale!
 The tawny-throated!
Hark! from that moonlit cedar what a burst!
 What triumph! hark—what pain!

 O wanderer from a Grecian shore,
Still, after many years, in distant lands,
Still nourishing in thy bewilder'd brain
That wild, unquench'd, deep-sunken, old-world pain—
 Say, will it never heal?
 And can this fragrant lawn
 With its cool trees, and night,
 And the sweet, tranquil Thames,
 And moonshine, and the dew,
 To thy rack'd heart and brain
  Afford no balm?

   Dost thou to-night behold,
Here, through the moonlight on this English grass,
The unfriendly palace in the Thracian wild?
   Dost thou again peruse
  With hot cheeks and sear'd eyes
  The too clear web, and thy dumb sister's shame?
   Dost thou once more assay
Thy flight, and feel come over thee,
Poor fugitive, the feathery change
Once more, and once more seem to make resound
With love and hate, triumph and agony,
Lone Daulis, and the high Cephissian vale?
   Listen, Eugenia—
How thick the bursts come crowding through the leaves!
   Again—thou hearest?
   Eternal passion!
    Eternal pain!

         (Matthew Arnold)

This is, perhaps, not quite a fair example, as it does have a great deal more formal symmetry than the majority of free verse poems. And yet even here there is a sense of a lack. It is as if, when watching a ballet, everything which is received from the union of music and movement should have to be supplied by watching the movement only. Free verse is emotional pattern without any regularity of sound pattern. It is of course nonsense to dismiss it as mere lawlessness. It can be as rigidly disciplined as the most complicated stanza construction, and it can bring the same complete satisfaction as the formal types of verse, but the sensitiveness of the reader must be far more specialized, and it is idle to pretend that the appeal of the free verse is, or ever can be, as general or as powerful as that of poetry where the emotional rhythm is matched by a regular rhythmical element in the sound pattern. And it is of interest to examine why this should be. What does the addition

of metre and rhyme add to poetry? The answer takes us
to one of the fundamental facts of human experience—
the compelling power of rhythmic regularity of move-
ment. It is an experience common to every human crea-
ture. Life is rooted in rhythm, and the great base of the
universal appeal of poetry must lie in its alliance to
the physiological bases of life itself—the rhythms of the
breath and the heart. Language with a regular rhyth-
mical time-beat has a peculiar power. It is at the same
time soothing and stimulating; sedative and tonic. An
enormous amount of poetry induces in the reader or
listener what is in reality a state of very light hypnosis:
it is literally 'entrancing'. The melody of its recurrent
time-beats induces this trance-like condition, and, at the
same time, by excluding all the associations of the every-
day world, all the disordered environment of 'dailiness',
it increases the emotional and sensuous susceptibilities,
and creates the condition known as hyper-aesthesia or
heightened sensibility. Our feelings get enclosed, by the
symmetrical recurrence of stress and sound in a charmed
circle, where they can live more fully and freely. All
very musical verse does this, but just as there are certain
drugs which in small doses are stimulants, but in large
doses are narcotics, so the music of words may pass the
stage of entrancement where certain faculties are stimu-
lated, and reach that stage where it is so soothing that
all are put to sleep, and the poet weaves a cradle of
words for his readers and rocks them in it. For example,
if a poem begins:

> Swiftly walk o'er the western wave,
>   Spirit of Night!
> Out of the misty eastern cave,
> Where, all the long and lone daylight,
> Thou wovest dreams of joy and fear,
> Which make thee terrible and dear,—
>   Swift be thy flight!

and is followed by only four more verses of that enchanting music, we can enjoy it to the full. But when a poem opens:

> Under yonder beech-tree single on the green-sward,
>   Couch'd with her arms behind her golden head,
> Knees and tresses folded to slip and ripple idly,
>   Lies my young love sleeping in the shade.
> Had I the heart to slide an arm beneath her,
>   Press her parting lips as her waist I gather slow,
> Waking in amazement she could not but embrace me:
>   Then would she hold me and never let me go?

and is followed by some thirty similar stanzas of rippling melody, the senses inevitably become blurred and comatose. It is as Swinburne wrote, in a stanza which is a just comment on much of his own poetry:

> A month or twain to live on honeycomb
> Is pleasant; but one tires of scented thyme,
> Cold sweet recurrence of accepted rhyme,
> And that strong purple under juice and foam
> Where the wine's heart has burst;
> Nor feel the latter kisses like the first.

Human powers of attentiveness, at any high degree of concentration, are indeed very limited, and the pleasures of poetry in all its aspects partake almost equally of what Coleridge calls the two master-movements or impulses of man—the love of uniformity and the love of variety. The effect of verbal rhythm on the nervous system is based on the creation of an appetite for a definitely recurring satisfaction, but unless the quality of that satisfaction is varied, it very soon ceases to satisfy. Four beat rhyming couplets, for example, become quite intolerable after a few lines:

> Sir Leoline, the Baron rich,
> Hath a toothless mastiff bitch;
> From her kennel beneath the rock
> She maketh answer to the clock....

and the varieties of stress and rhythm which Coleridge introduces in *Christabel* are almost endless.

> Is the night chilly and dark?
> The night is chilly, but not dark.
> The thin gray cloud is spread on high,
> It covers but not hides the sky.
> The moon is behind, and at the full;
> And yet she looks both small and dull,
> The night is chill, the cloud is gray:
> 'Tis a month before the month of May,
> And the spring comes slowly up this way.

To win the full response of the reader the poetic artist so manipulates the sequence of his syllables that his verbal rhythm, his time-beat, is never absolutely regular for long. He creates a certain anticipation in the reader's mind, and metrical effects are all built up on the basis of an anticipated recurrent sound pattern, but as I. A. Richards says: 'most rhythms are made up as much of disappointments and postponements and surprises and betrayals as of simple straightforward satisfactions.'

ON TIME

> Fly envious Time, till thou run out thy race,
> Call on the lazy leaden-stepping hours,
> Whose speed is but the heavy Plummets pace;
> And glut thyself with what thy womb devours,
> Which is no more than what is false and vain,
> And merely mortal dross;
> So little is our loss,
> So little is thy gain.

For when as each thing bad thou hast entomb'd,
And last of all, thy greedy self consum'd,
Then long Eternity shall greet our bliss
With an individual kiss;
And Joy shall overtake us as a flood,
When everything that is sincerely good
And perfectly divine,
With Truth, and Peace, and Love shall ever shine
About the supreme Throne
Of him t' whose happy-making sight alone,
When once our heav'nly-guided soul shall climb,
Then all this earthy grossness quit,
Attir'd with Stars we shall for ever sit,
   Triumphing over Death, and Chance, and thee
     O Time.

(John Milton)

A living regular rhythm is like the rhythm of the waves of the sea, a rhythm of infinite variety in uniformity, not the rhythm of the ticking of a clock. The metre provides an external symmetry, but within that symmetry the sound movement can have every variety of flexible treatment.

3.

THE history of poetry is the history of the perpetual discovery by poets of fresh ways in which they can manipulate rhythmical effects, and of those effects in turn becoming artificial, and again provoking further experiment and revolt. For artificiality is as great an enemy of poetic satisfaction as monotony. Take a poem all dewy freshness and debonair daintiness and spontaneity like Skelton's *To Mistress Margaret Hussey:*

Merry Margaret
As midsummer flower,
Gentle as falcon
Or hawk of the tower:

> With solace and gladness,
> Much mirth and no madness,
> All good and no badness;
> > So joyously,
> > So maidenly,
> > So womanly
> > Her demeaning;
> > In everything,
> > Far, far passing
> > That I can indite,
> > Or suffice to write
> Of Merry Margaret
> As midsummer flower,
> Gentle as falcon
> Or hawk of the tower

and put it beside a famous poem of Tennyson, beautiful indeed, but where the beauty has no shadow of that spontaneity and freshness: where we feel that each line, each word, each syllable and each letter has been placed deliberately with the most consummate craftsmanship.

COME DOWN, O MAID

Come down, O maid, from yonder mountain height:
What pleasure lives in height (the shepherd sang),
In height and cold, the splendour of the hills?
But cease to move so near the Heavens, and cease
To glide a sunbeam by the blasted Pine,
To sit a star upon the sparkling spire;
And come, for Love is of the valley, come,
For Love is of the valley, come thou down
And find him; by the happy threshold, he,
Or hand in hand with Plenty in the maize,
Or red with spirted purple of the vats,
Or foxlike in the vine; nor cares to walk
With Death and Morning on the silver horns,
Nor wilt thou snare him in the white ravine,
Nor find him dropt upon the firths of ice,

That huddling slant in furrow-cloven falls
To roll the torrent out of dusky doors;
But follow; let the torrent dance thee down
To find him in the valley; let the wild
Lean-headed Eagles yelp alone, and leave
The monstrous ledges there to slope, and spill
Their thousand wreaths of dangling water-smoke,
That like a broken purpose waste in air:
So waste not thou; but come; for all the vales
Await thee; azure pillars of the hearth
Arise to thee; the children call, and I
Thy shepherd pipe, and sweet is every sound,
Sweeter thy voice, but every sound is sweet;
Myriads of rivulets hurrying thro' the lawn,
The moan of doves in immemorial elms,
And murmuring of innumerable bees.

It is marvellously done, and yet it is on the whole unsatisfying. It is the type of poetry one tires of very soon. It lacks body and blood and brain. It has neither impersonal strength nor personal passion. It is *too* musical, *too* sweet, *too* fluid, *too* flexible.

At the other extreme, we can find rhythms which are too rigid, too strong: verse which is muscle-bound with excess of discipline and over-development in one direction. Some of the choruses in *Samson Agonistes,* for example:

Many are the sayings of the wise
In ancient and in modern books enroll'd;
Extolling Patience as the truest fortitude;
And to the bearing well of all calamities,
All chances incident to man's frail life
Consolations writ
With studied argument, and much persuasion
        sought
Lenient of grief and anxious thought,
But with th' afflicted in his pangs their sound
Little prevails, or rather seems a tune,

> Harsh, and of dissonant mood from his com-
>   plaint,
> Unless he feel within
> Some source of consolation from above;
> Secret refreshings, that repair his strength,
> And fainting spirits uphold.

Here the poet has created so intensely specialized an in-
tellectual rhythm that it has stifled the life out of the
natural rhythms of the English language.

4.

RHYME still further accentuates the functions of metre.
Its chime satisfies the ear in a peculiar way of its own,
and it plays a definitely constructive purpose in the
architecture of the poem. It has a binding quality, which
can by itself alone almost unify a poem:

> What hadst thou to do being born,
>   Mother, when winds were at ease,
> As a flower of the springtime of corn,
>   A flower of the foam of the seas?
> For bitter thou wast from thy birth,
>   Aphrodite, a mother of strife;
> For before thee some rest was on earth,
>   A little respite from tears,
> A little pleasure of life;
> For life was not then as thou art,
>   But as one that waxeth in years
> Sweet-spoken, a fruitful wife;
>   Earth had no thorn, and desire
> No sting, neither death any dart;
>   What hadst thou to do amongst these,
>   Thou, clothed with a burning fire,
> Thou, girt with sorrow of heart,
>   Thou, sprung of the seed of the seas
> As an ear from a seed of corn,
>   As a brand plucked forth of a pyre,

As a ray shed forth of the morn,
    For division of soul and disease,
For a dart and a sting and a thorn?
What ailed thee then to be born?
                    (Algernon Charles Swinburne)

But the most important function of rhyme beyond its
musical one, is that it places the experience communi-
cated by the words still further from 'dailiness', creat-
ing as it were a kind of frame around it which isolates
it. This is carried further still if it is accompanied by a
recurrent refrain, which acts again as an aid to poetic
hypnosis. The refrain may intensify the general theme
of the poem, as in Kipling's *Recessional*, or it may have
nothing to do with the poem. In many old songs and
ballads it is mere nonsense, but it reminds the reader he
is in another world and keeps him there.

It was a lover and his lass,
    With a hey, and a ho, and a hey nonino,
That o'er the green corn-field did pass,
    In the spring time, the only pretty ring time,
When birds do sing, hey ding a ding, ding;
Sweet lovers love the spring.

Between the acres of the rye,
    With a hey, and a ho, and a hey nonino,
These pretty country folks would lie,
    In the spring time, the only pretty ring time,
When birds do sing, hey ding a ding, ding;
Sweet lovers love the spring.

This carol they began that hour,
    With a hey, and a ho, and a hey nonino,
How that life was but a flower
    In the spring time, the only pretty ring time,
When birds do sing, hey ding a ding, ding;
Sweet lovers love the spring.

And, therefore, take the present time
With a hey, and a ho, and a hey nonino,
For love is crownèd with the prime
In the spring time, the only pretty ring time,
When birds do sing, hey ding a ding, ding;
Sweet lovers love the spring.

(William Shakespeare)

The use of repetition, which is here merely melody and light-heartedness, may, of course, become a sophisticated use, where the artist consciously builds up an emotional and musical effect from an irregular and subtle sound pattern of recurrent syllables.

And on what beautiful morning
With the sun shining and the sea calling
Shall I awake?
Shall I give up my unsubstantial sword
And go down to the water,
With all the trumpets sounding,
And with tears and laughter
Take
The white hand of my Lord?
Oh, on what beautiful morning
Shall I awake,
And bathing in the blue river
Forget the very dark night,
This night, for ever?
On what beautiful morning?

(T. H. White)

5.

THERE is a wealth of material for study in all the details of the poet's deliberate rhythmic craftsmanship. For, as Touchstone said, 'the truest poetry is the most feigning', and the effects which we sometimes loosely term 'magical' do not come by chance, or sorcery. There is the whole question of *tempo* for instance: the subject

of pauses, when the verbal experience goes underground
as it were and comes up again—that natural lingering
of the voice which D. H. Lawrence speaks of. Silence
may play fully as important a part as sound in the rhyth-
mic pattern. Or again, there is the consideration of the
effects which depend on variation of pitch within the
poem itself. As an example take the first three lines of
one of Wordsworth's sonnets:

> Surprized by joy—impatient as the Wind
> I turned to share the transport—oh! with whom
> But Thee, deep buried in the silent tomb. . . .

Here the poet strikes a high, full note of rapture, then
there is a pause, weighted with rhythmic suspense, fol-
lowed by a line in which a falling cadence lowers the
pitch almost word by word.

There is the question, too, of why certain variations
of sound pattern seem for some reason to have a pecul-
iarly pleasurable effect on the sensory nerves. The juxta-
position of a long and a short line is one of them. It is
a powerful emotional stimulant. Keats's lines on seeing
a lock of Milton's hair is a good example:

> A lock of thy bright hair,—
> Sudden it came,
> And I was startled, when I caught thy name
> Coupled so unaware.

Or Browning's *Love among the Ruins,* or those very
moving verses of R. L. Stevenson:

> Blows the wind today, and the sun and the rain are flying,
> Blows the wind on the moors today and now,
> Where about the graves of the martyrs the whaups are crying,
> My heart remembers how!

Be it granted me to behold you again in dying,
    Hills of home! and to hear again the call:
Hear about the graves of the martyrs the peewees crying,
    And hear no more at all.

The *texture* of language is again of vital importance
in the total effect of sound value and emotional flavour.
Compare it in a verse from Francis Thompson's *The
Hound of Heaven,* with its deliberate use of words
loaded with suggestions of the strange, the rich, the rare
and the remote; and a verse from Donne's *A Hymn to
Christ,* with its deliberate striving to embody the
rhythms of speech into vehement, impassioned poetry.

Across the margent of the world I fled,
    And troubled the gold gateways of the stars,
    Smiting for shelter on their clangèd bars;
        Fretted to dulcet jars
And silvern chatter the pale ports o' the moon.
I said to dawn: Be sudden; to eve: Be soon;
    With thy young skyey blossoms heap me over
        From this tremendous Lover!

*

Nor thou nor thy religion dost control,
The amorousness of an harmonious Soul,
But thou would'st have that love thyself: As thou
Art jealous, Lord, so I am jealous now,
Thou lov'st not, till from loving more, thou free
My soul: Who ever gives, takes liberty:
    O, if thou car'st not whom I love
        Alas, thou lov'st not me.

Or there is the whole enormous subject of the effects
which can be gained by the skilled use of the relation
between certain varieties of vowels and consonants. How
Milton, for instance, can create a sense of intolerable
sadness by the repetition of certain similar sound values.

But O the heavy change, now thou art *gone,*
Now thou art *gone,* and never must *return!*
Thee, Shepherd, thee the woods and desert caves,
With wild thyme and the gadding vine o'er*grown*
And all their echoes *mourn.*

Or how Herrick can make the music of Julia's voice live
exquisitely in the soft sibilants and liquid syllables in
which he sings of it.

So smooth, so sweet, so silv'ry is thy voice,
As, could they hear, the Damn'd would make no
noise,
But listen to thee (walking in thy chamber)
Melting melodious words, to lutes of amber.

Or how Donne, again, can make the variations on the
letter 'o' toll like a bell through a whole stanza.

Poor soul, in this thy flesh what dost thou know?
Thou know'st thyself so little that thou know'st not
How thou did'st die, nor how thou wast begot.
Thou neither know'st how thou at first camest in,
Nor how thou took'st the poison of man's sin;
Nor dost thou, though thou know'st that thou art
so
By what way thou art made immortal know.

6.

So much for a few details only, for this subject is an
endless one. In conclusion, let us take a few illustrations
of the perfect marriage of matter and manner, of poetic
design which is the perfect communication of the intel-
lectual and emotional pattern in the heart of the poet's
experience.

THE PARTING

Since there's no help, come let us kiss and part—
Nay I have done, you get no more of me;
And I am glad, yes, glad with all my heart,
That thus so cleanly I myself can free.
Shake hands for ever, cancel all our vows,
And when we meet at any time again,
Be it not seen in either of our brows
That we one jot of former love retain.
Now at the last gasp of Love's latest breath,
When, his pulse failing, Passion speechless lies,
When Faith is kneeling by his bed of death,
And Innocence is closing up his eyes,
　　—Now if thou would'st, when all have given
　　　　him over,
　　From death to life thou might'st him yet recover.
　　　　　　　　　　　　　　(Michael Drayton)

Here it is not the actual music of the syllables which concerns us, but the skill of the dramatic movement within the sonnet form. The semi-conversational flavour of the first eight lines, created by the use of colloquialisms such as 'there's no help', 'you get no more of me', 'shake hands for ever', 'jot', and suggesting the tone of detached indifference in the 'hero'. Then the change in the whole movement of the rhythm as emotion vanquishes common-sense, so that the whole tone and texture of the language is modified, poetic symbolism replacing colloquialism, and flowing musical lines replacing the choppy rhythms of speech. And at the end, the semi-ironic, semi-triumphant couplet with no music at all, which, although it gives a completely new twist to the thought, yet resolves all that has gone before into a unifying final chord.

THE SOLITARY REAPER

Behold her, single in the field,
   Yon solitary Highland Lass!
Reaping and singing by herself;
   Stop here, or gently pass!
Alone she cuts and binds the grain,
And sings a melancholy strain;
O listen! for the Vale profound
Is overflowing with the sound.

No Nightingale did ever chaunt
   More welcome notes to weary bands
Of travellers in some shady haunt,
   Among Arabian sands:
A voice so thrilling ne'er was heard
In spring-time from the Cuckoo-bird,
Breaking the silence of the seas
Among the farthest Hebrides.

Will no one tell me what she sings?—
   Perhaps the plaintive numbers flow
For old, unhappy, far-off things,
   And battles long ago:
Or is it some more humble lay,
Familiar matter of to-day?
Some natural sorrow, loss, or pain,
That has been, and may be again?

Whate'er the theme, the Maiden sang
   As if her song could have no ending;
I saw her singing at her work,
   And o'er the sickle bending;—
I listen'd, motionless, and still;
And, as I mounted up the hill,
The music in my heart I bore,
Long after it was heard no more.

              (William Wordsworth)

This exquisitely perfect poem, though its beauty captures the heart at once in its entirety and seems at first sight utterly simple, repays a closer analysis, for it is an example of the most complex ordering and harmonizing and unifying of material. There is the central picture of that unforgettable solitary figure reaping and singing. She is always there, throughout, but what riches of the heart are blended and harmonized with that picture! Everything that plaintive, lovely voice suggests of music, of refreshment, of the remote, the romantic, the mysterious, the enchanting: everything it suggests, too, of 'the still sad music of humanity': everything of the immortal and the eternal which the poet felt in that vision, and which he translated into the eternity and immortality of art.

And for all this, he has found the haunting, inevitable words.

> O listen, for the Vale profound
> Is overflowing with the sound.
>
> Breaking the silence of the seas
> Among the farthest Hebrides.
>
> ... old unhappy far-off things
> And battles long ago.
>
> I saw her singing at her work
> And o'er the sickle bending;—

There is no comment to be made on such lines. They bring that complete and absolute satisfaction and certainty and fulfilment which we call perfect beauty.

If we compare *The Solitary Reaper* with another masterpiece with some points in common with it, Keats's *La Belle Dame Sans Merci,* we can see something of the way two different artists work.

'O what can ail thee, knight-at-arms,
    Alone and palely loitering?
The sedge is wither'd from the lake,
    And no birds sing.

'O what can ail thee, knight-at-arms,
    So haggard and so woe-begone?
The squirrel's granary is full,
    And the harvest's done.

'I see a lily on thy brow
    With anguish moist and fever dew;
And on thy cheek a fading rose
    Fast withereth too.'

'I met a lady in the meads,
    Full beautiful--a faery's child,
Her hair was long, her foot was light,
    And her eyes were wild.

'I made a garland for her head,
    And bracelets too, and fragrant zone;
She look'd at me as she did love,
    And made sweet moan.

'I set her on my pacing steed
    And nothing else saw all day long,
For sideways would she lean, and sing
    A faery's song.

'She found me roots of relish sweet,
    And honey wild and manna dew
And sure in language strange she said,
    "I love thee true!"

'She took me to her elfin grot,
    And there she wept and sigh'd full sore;
And there I shut her wild, wild eyes
    With kisses four.

'And there she lullèd me asleep
   And there I dream'd—Ah! woe betide!
The latest dream I ever dream'd
   On the cold hill's side.

'I saw pale kings and princes too,
   Pale warriors, death-pale were they all;
Who cried—"La belle Dame sans Merci
   Hath thee in thrall!"

'I saw their starved lips in the gloam
   With horrid warning gapèd wide,
And I awoke and found me here
   On the cold hill's side.

'And this is why I sojourn here
   Alone and palely loitering,
Though the sedge is wither'd from the lake,
   And no birds sing.'

Both poets build round a central picture—a picture, isolated and framed in a metrical sound pattern of extreme beauty and simplicity and purity of outline. Both use words with a magic and music which belong only to the great poetic masters; but whereas Wordsworth fuses his unity from the most diverse and varied elements, harmonizing the world of the beholder and of the singer, of romance and reality, of the temporal and the visionary, Keats unifies his by rigidly excluding anything which does not directly contribute to the vividness of the peculiar atmosphere he is intent on creating. Wordsworth keeps us in the real world and enriches it with suggestions which call responses from a multitude of hidden springs; Keats compels us to be withdrawn completely into his dream-world, and bewitches us there in the charmed circle of its own experience. His background, his series of scenes, his choice of detail and his actual vocabulary and use of words make it as impossible for the reader to escape the intensity of his spell, as it was for the knight to escape that of *la belle dame*.

ON A DEAD CHILD

Perfect little body, without fault or stain on thee,
   With promise of strength and manhood full and fair!
     Though cold and stark and bare,
The bloom and the charm of life doth awhile remain on thee.

Thy mother's treasure wert thou;—alas! no longer
   To visit her heart with wondrous joy; to be
     Thy father's pride;—ah, he
Must gather his faith together, and his strength make
     stronger.

To me, as I move thee now in the last duty,
   Dost thou with a turn or gesture anon respond;
     Startling my fancy fond
With a chance attitude of the head, a freak of beauty.

Thy hand clasps, as 'twas wont, my finger, and holds it:
   But the grasp is the clasp of Death, heartbreaking and stiff;
     Yet feels to my hand as if
'Twas still thy will, thy pleasure and trust that enfolds it.

So I lay thee there, thy sunken eyelids closing,—
   Go lie thou there in thy coffin, thy last little bed!—
     Propping thy wise, sad head,
Thy firm, pale hands across thy chest disposing.

So quiet! doth the change content thee?—Death, whither hath
     he taken thee?
   To a world, do I think, that rights the disaster of this?
     The vision of which I miss,
Who weep for the body, and wish but to warm thee and
     awaken thee?

Ah! little at best can all our hopes avail us
   To lift this sorrow, or cheer us, when in the dark,
     Unwilling, alone we embark,
And the things we have seen and have known and have
     heard of, fail us.

                   (Robert Bridges)

This is another poem which, compared with the two last, illustrates the difference between personal and impersonal rhythms. It is impossible to detach this from the personality of the poet who created it, just as it is impossible to detach *The Folly of Being Comforted*. Although it is governed by a regular metrical arrangement, the organic movement seems to create its own verbal rhythms in each verse, blending the cadences of speech and the vocabulary of poetry in a way all its own. It ebbs and flows from the concrete to the abstract, from the physical to the emotional and the intellectual, and in spite of the summing up of the last verse, it concludes nothing. Its being streams on in the heart and mind after it has ended, its questions groping in human darkness, its conclusions beating impotently in the air... There is no sense of fulfilment, of serenity, of completion: it is a most exquisite presentation of an emotion which refuses to be serene and complete. For it is not the picture of the dead child which is the thing of supreme importance to the poet, but the eternal mystery which arises from it.

IMAGERY

I.

WHEN Sir Philip Sidney, in *The Defence of Poesie*, is championing the art he loved so well, he speaks of 'that exquisite observing of number and measure in words, and that high-flying liberty of conceit proper to the poet.' We have already said something of the exquisite observing of number and measure, but we have not yet discussed his high-flying liberty of conceit. And without all that Sidney means by that, poetry is unthinkable. As he says again: 'Imaging is in itself the very height and life of poetry.'

It must be so, from the very nature of the poetic vision, which, as we saw in the first chapter, always embodies itself in the form of symbols. The personality of the poet, which is the well-spring of his poetry, is fed by innumerable streams and channels of consciousness: by all that he has lived and suffered and enjoyed; all that he has observed and experienced by his senses; all that he has read of other men's creation and which has become part of his own being; all that he has reasoned and speculated upon. His poetry will be a world created from all that he has known and felt and seen and heard and thought, and his image-making poetic faculty, his 'imagination', will blend together his memories and his immediate perceptions into a thousand varieties of shapes and associations of living loveliness and power.

> Dust as we are, the immortal spirit grows
> Like harmony in music; there is a dark
> Inscrutable workmanship that reconciles
> Discordant elements, makes them cling together
> In one society.

All language in common use is figurative, and we all use imagery all day long in our daily speech. However apparently direct and unadorned the poet makes his verses, he will inevitably employ images. However simple his statement he cannot make it abstract.

> Had we never lov'd sae kindly,
> Had we never lov'd sae blindly,
> Never met—or never parted,
> We had ne'er been broken-hearted.

Even here, in spite of the simplicity of the statement, there are three figurative expressions—*kindly, blindly,* and *broken-hearted,* in the four lines. But the poet does not only make use of images which have become common currency in language, he perpetually discovers others which hold in their outline or suggestion or inter-relation, the power to convey the unique flavour which he seeks to evoke. He will not say 'evening brings twi-light', but

> Thy dewy fingers draw
> The gradual dusky veil.

He will not say 'I was afraid', but

> Fear at my heart, as at a cup
> My life-blood seem'd to sip!

Instead of declaring his poetry to be that of a soldier he says his Muse

> Tempers her words to trampling horses' feet.

Instead of praying for peace and faith and hope, he cries,

> Give me my scallop-shell of quiet,
>   My staff of faith to walk upon,
> My scrip of joy, immortal diet,
>   My bottle of salvation,
> My gown of glory, hope's true gage;
> And thus I'll take my pilgrimage.

The bad poet no less than the good is marked by the use he makes of images. When he attempts to describe the mystery of transubstantiation he will say,

> The modest water saw its God and blushed.

And he will write as the epitaph on a young girl,

> So, though a virgin, yet a bride
> To every grace, she justified
> A chaste polygamy, and died.

The poet's creation of images ranges from the simplest use of personification (as in the two first examples above) or of simile, to the most complex use of symbolism and metaphor. It may be just an illustration, or a comment through comparison, of the poet's theme. 'William tired himself seeking an epithet for the cuckoo,' writes Dorothy Wordsworth in her journal, and it is invariably a quality of the poetic mind that it seeks and seizes relationships, and works by the perceptions of analogies, likening the abstract to the concrete or the concrete to the abstract, or one abstraction to another abstraction, or one concrete thing to another concrete thing, as it clarifies and evokes different qualities of experience.

> Let us go then, you and I
> When the evening is spread out against the sky
> Like a patient etherized upon a table.

*

Music that gentlier on the spirit lies,
Than tired eyelids upon tired eyes.

*

Mild as a star in water.

*

The winds, that will be howling at all hours,
And are up-gathered now like sleeping flowers.

*

The Champak odours fail
Like sweet thoughts in a dream.

*

The wild tulip, at end of its tube, blows out its great red bell
Like a thin clear bubble of blood.

*

Her goodly eyes lyke Saphyres shining bright,
Her forehead yvory white,
Her cheekes lyke apples which the sun hath rudded,
Her lips lyke cherryes charming men to byte,
Her brest lyke to a bowle of creame uncrudded,
Her paps lyke lyllies budded,
Her snowie necke lyke to a marble towre;
And all her body like a pallace fayre,
Ascending up, with many a stately stayre,
To honors seat and chastities sweet bowre.

But the simple, straightforward illustration of the
quality of one thing by likening it to another is a very
small corner of the poet's use of imagery, and in its
more subtle and intricate forms the image becomes, not
a mere comment on, or illustration of, the poet's theme
—a trimming to it, as it were—but woven into its very
texture, as the image of discovery and exploration was
woven into the texture of Keats's experience of reading

Homer, or as the images of travel and of warfare are woven into the idea of the poet's rejoining of his dead wife in Henry King's *The Exequy*.

> Sleep on my Love in thy cold bed
> Never to be disquieted!
> My last good night! Thou wilt not wake
> Till I thy fate shall overtake:
>
> . . . . . .
>
> Stay for me there; I will not fail
> To meet thee in that hollow Vale.
> And think not much of my delay;
> I am already on the way,
> And follow thee with all the speed
> Desire can make, or sorrows breed.
> Each minute is a short degree,
> And ev'ry hour a step towards thee.
> At night when I betake to rest,
> Next morn I rise nearer my West
> Of life, almost by eight hours sail,
> Than when sleep breath'd his drowsy gale.
>
> . . . . . .
>
> 'Tis true, with shame and grief I yield,
> Thou like the Van first took'st the field,
> And gotten hast the victory
> In thus adventuring to die
> Before me, whose more years might crave
> A just precedence in the grave.
> But hark! My Pulse like a soft Drum
> Beats my approach, tells Thee I come;
> And slow howe'er my marches be,
> I shall at last sit down by Thee.

As it is very clearly illustrated here, the whole mode of vision in which the theme is seen and felt is conditioned by the symbols and images it has suggested; and they are the means of creating the special emotion which accompanies it, and enriches it. Indeed that sense of revelation which illumines the reader of great poetry bursts upon him more brightly from the poet's use of metaphor than from any of the other uses of language. As Aristotle said, it is the one thing which cannot be learnt from others. It would be a sufficient disproof of the definition of genius as the infinite capacity for taking pains, that no amount of taking pains could result in thinking of lines such as:

> Thou still unravish'd bride of quietness.
> Bare ruin'd choirs where late the sweet birds sang.
> Now lies the Earth all Danaé to the stars.

2.

How imagery comes to the poet, how it is 'carried alive into the heart by passion' is, ultimately, too mysterious a process to analyze. It brings us back at once to the problem of creation in general. Under the influence of the creative ferment the consciousness of the poet seizes associations—or is seized by them, for the process of association is always partly unconscious—and poetry is the union of the mental and emotional excitement of the experience with the imagery which leaps to meet it, and which must be already in the memory of the poet. Wordsworth says the poet's influxes of feeling are modified and directed by his thoughts, which are the representatives of all his past feelings, and Coleridge speaks of 'the streamy nature of association, which thinking curbs and rudders'. There is obviously the final conscious act of the choice and handling of the material, but that streamy nature of association leads us back to the mysterious source and fountain of the poetic process and to all the mazy meanderings and tributaries, to all the changes and modifications and accretions which the poet's original experience receives in the course of becoming a poem.

It is better, therefore, to try and understand something of the effects of imagery upon the sensitive reader —what imagery *does*—than to try and probe to the secrets of its inception.

One of the great functions of poetry, as I have said before, is to awaken the dead. The poet brings life to the spirit of his reader by quickening his consciousness of language, by making words alive. The conventional vocabulary of the average liver of life slips through the well-worn channels of response without enough friction to provoke any real awareness of it at all. It is like the effect of the cocks' crowing on the milkman compared with their effect on the poet, in Edward Thomas's poem.

COCKCROW

Out of the wood of thoughts that grow by night
To be cut down by the sharp ax of light,—
Out of the night, two cocks together crow,
Cleaving the darkness with a silver blow:
And bright before my eyes twin trumpeters stand,
Heralds of splendour, one at either hand,
Each facing each as in a coat of arms;—
The milkers lace their boots up at the farms.

But just as the poet's response to experience is not only finer and fuller but different from that of the average liver of life, so must he find a use of language, which is not only finer and fuller, but is also different, to communicate his response: He finds imagery. 'When the sun rises, do you not see a round disk of fire something like a guinea?' said a practical minded friend to Blake. And the poet replied: 'Oh no, I see an immeasurable company of the heavenly host crying Holy Holy Holy is the Lord God Almighty.' It is the translation of this type of vision into language which brings that blending of surprise and satisfaction, that shock to the nerve centres followed by a new co-ordination in them, which is the thrill of poetry.

This does not mean that the more images a poet uses, the better is the poetry he writes, as these verses by Robert Southwell will show.

> The loppèd tree in time may grow again,
> Most naked plants renew both fruit and flower;
> The sorest wight may find release of pain,
> The driest soil suck in some moist'ning shower;
> Times go by turns and chances change by course,
> From foul to fair, from better hap to worse.
>
> The sea of Fortune doth not ever flow,
> She draws her favours to the lowest ebb;
> Her tides hath equal times to come and go
> Her loom doth weave the fine and coarsest web;
> No joy so great but runneth to an end,
> No hap so hard but may in fine amend.
>
> Not always fall of leaf nor ever spring,
> No endless night yet not eternal day;
> The saddest birds a season find to sing,
> The roughest storm a calm may soon allay:
> Thus with succeeding turns God tempereth all,
> That man may hope to rise, yet fear to fall.

Here is a poem (there is yet another verse at the end) which is composed almost entirely of images, but whose whole effect is of the utmost dullness and flatness because the use of the figurative language never rises beyond that of simple illustration. The original theme, not very profound anyhow, is smothered under a load of simile and metaphor all as commonplace as the thought itself, and the reader soon feels smothered too. It is a collection of parts added each to each in a line or piled one on top of the other, instead of coalescing into a pattern by inter-relation and inter-dependence. Let us compare it with two stanzas from Shelley's *The Cloud*.

> That orbèd maiden with white fire laden
>   Whom mortals call the Moon,
> Glides glimmering o'er my fleece-like floor,
>   By the midnight breezes strewn;
> And wherever the beat of her unseen feet,
>   Which only the angels hear,
> May have broken the woof of my tent's thin roof,
>   The stars peep behind her and peer;
> And I laugh to see them whirl and flee,
>   Like a swarm of golden bees,
> When I widen the rent in my wind-built tent,
>   Till the calm rivers, lakes and seas,
> Like strips of the sky fallen through me on high
>   Are each paved with the moon and these.
>
> I bind the Sun's throne with a burning zone,
>   And the Moon's with a girdle of pearl;
> The volcanoes are dim, and the stars reel and swim,
>   When the whirlwinds my banner unfurl.
> From cape to cape, with a bridge-like shape,
>   Over a torrent sea,
> Sunbeam-proof, I hang like a roof,—
>   The mountains its columns be.
> The triumphal arch through which I march
>   With hurricane, fire and snow,
> When the Powers of the air are chained to my chair,
>   Is the million-coloured bow;
> The sphere-fire above its soft colours wove,
>   While the moist earth was laughing below.

Here the imagery does not ornament or illustrate or overlay the theme: it is an inseparable part of the theme. It *is* the theme. Its richness and lightness and delicacy, its airy diaphanous texture and glancing sheen, carry the whole quality of the poem in themselves. We cannot justly say it is too varied and elaborate, since it is of its

very essence to be varied and elaborate; and the details
of its variety and elaboration are welded into a poetic
structure which, in spite of the fragility of its materials,
is a unity in which each part contributes to the whole
conception and is in vital relationship with it.

Coleridge has best summed up the essentials of the
matter.

'Images, however faithfully copied from Nature, and
as accurately represented in words, do not of themselves
characterize the poet. They become proofs of genius
only in so far as they are modified by a predominant
passion, or by associated thoughts and images awakened
by that passion: or when they have the effect of reduc-
ing multitude to unity, or succession to an instant: or
lastly, when a human and intellectual life is transferred
to them from the poet's own spirit.'

Such a completely simple figure, for example, as 'a
slumber did my spirit seal' in the Lucy poem we have
already quoted, is so essential a part of the whole poem
that the emotions and sensations and even the visual sug-
gestions aroused by it vibrate through the eight lines and
provide the unifying idea of the whole. Not only does
the image completely sum up the emotional sense of the
poet's blind confidence and sense of security in his hap-
piness, in the first verse, but the actual vision it evokes
of immobility and closed eyelids and sealed ears becomes
identified at once in the second verse with Lucy's eternal
sleep of death.

Not that it is by any means always necessary for the
full effect of an image—or even advisable—that the
reader should have any very clear visual outline of it.
Imagine making a clear mental picture of Tennyson's
verse

Who breaks his birth's invidious bar
And grasps the skirts of happy chance,
And breasts the blows of circumstance,
And grapples with his evil star.

In any case, this is not a very happy fusion of ideas, but even in the finest poetry, the imagery need never be exact at all, for factual truth may bear the same relation to emotional truth, as a slow motion picture of a horse jumping bears to the sense of exhilaration felt when one watches him fly over a hurdle. The factual detail and the total effect may be quite different, even completely contradictory. For instance, when Shakespeare writes,

When to the Sessions of sweet silent thought
I summon up remembrance of things past,

no visualization of the image, as a scene in a court of law, is possible if we are to seize its abstract emotional value: the experience is entirely a business of the spirit. And in Donne's *A Valediction Forbidding Mourning* there is a famous image which is a constant source of disagreement among readers. The poet is urging to his beloved that their parting is not really a division.

Our two souls therefore, which are one
Though I must go, endure not yet
A breach, but an expansion,
Like gold to airy thinness beat.

If they be two, they are two so
As stiff twin compasses are two;
Thy soul, the fix'd foot, makes no show
To move, but doth, if th'other do.

And though it in the centre sit,
Yet, when the other far doth roam,
It leans, and hearkens after it,
And grows erect, as that comes home.

> Such wilt thou be to me, who must
> Like th'other foot, obliquely run;
> Thy firmness makes my circle just,
> And makes me end where I begun.

To the too concretely minded reader the actual vision of the pair of compasses, the facts that they are stiff and metallic and connected perhaps with unpleasant memories of school days and geometry, destroys the emotional value of the image. But they should not be conceived visually at all. What the poet is concerned with is the *feel* of a pair of compasses, that sense of leaning and firmness and the 'pull' between the two feet, and the translation of those sensations into emotional terms.

When we come to examine more complex uses of imagery, it is an ever-recurrent surprise to discover the power poetry has to assimilate and unify the diversity of material which the streamy nature of association sweeps into the poet's conscious mind. In any elaborate organization of figurative language nothing has merely its face value. A poem is never the sum total of its individual parts any more than a face is the sum total of its individual features. It is the relationships of the various images which create the poem, the way they colour and influence each other, the way in which a wide variety of different kinds of objects, of suggestions, of perceptions are subdued to one predominant idea, while at the same time they enrich it with a host of subsidiary ideas proper to each. Take one of Shakespeare's sonnets (XC), on the theme that if the poet is to lose his friend, he would rather the blow came at once, while he is already in disgrace with fortune.

> Then hate me when thou wilt; if ever, now;
> Now, while the world is bent my deeds to cross,
> Join with the spite of fortune, make me bow,
> And do not drop in for an after-loss:

Ah, do not, when my heart hath 'scaped this sorrow,
Come in the rearward of a conquer'd woe;
Give not a windy night a rainy morrow,
To linger out a purposed overthrow.
If thou wilt leave me, do not leave me last,
When other petty griefs have done their spite,
But in the onset come: so shall I taste
At first the very worst of fortune's might;
    And other strains of woe, which now seem woe,
    Compared with loss of thee will not seem so.

Image after image is called up: suggestions of human
malignancy and of the sport of fortune, of a late visitor
'dropping in' when others have left, of escape, of an
army overtaken in flight, of the English climate, of
wrestling, of keeping a tit-bit to eat at the end—all
jumbled together, abstract and concrete jostling each
other—a mingling of elaborate 'poetic diction' with
common colloquialisms. And yet the whole is an indi-
visible unity.

In very concentrated and closely interlocked imagery
such as this, it is not possible for the reader to give a
completely rational account of his responses. Or take
the octave of Hopkins' sonnet *The Windhover*.

I caught this morning morning's minion, Kingdom of day-
    light's dauphin, dapple-dawn-drawn Falcon, in his
    riding
Of the rolling level underneath him steady air, and striding
High there, how he rung upon the rein of a wimpling wing
In his ecstasy! then off, off forth on swing,
    As a skate's heel sweeps smooth on a bow-bend: the hurl and
    gliding
Rebuffed the big wind. My heart in hiding
Stirred for a bird,—the achieve of, the mastery of the
    thing!

Leaving aside various subtleties in the use of the language bearing on the whole theme of the poem, which we are not discussing here, how much has been packed into the first six and a half lines to give us that stirring sense summed up in 'the achieve of, the mastery of the thing!' After the bird itself has swept into our vision on the wings of the joy of the morning, there are four independent images to give cumulative force to the impression, and though they do give this cumulative force, they do so in a most surprising way, for they present independent and contradictory pictures. There is the gorgeous flash of his riding 'the rolling level underneath him steady air', swerving on a wimpling wing as if reined to one side: and at the same time he is striding, sweeping and swinging on skates, and hurling and gliding against the wind. But there is no sense whatever of confusion of effect. In some mysterious way each image has clear independent life, even if it is only half-unfolded and developed, while at the same time it loses all sharpness of identity in the general emotional colour of the whole.

This passage, indeed, illustrates very well every point in Coleridge's analysis of the way in which genius handles images. We see them modified by a predominant emotion, reducing multitude to unity and succession to an instant, and finally, having human and intellectual life transferred to them from the poet's own spirit. The rhythm and moulding of the figurative language in those lines are the result of an individual and inimitable manner of emotional perception, and could belong to no other spirit than that of Hopkins.

This last quality, the irradiation of imagery by a personality, is the vaguest and most elusive to define, but the most unmistakable possession of the great poet, and it is the achievement by which poetry proves triumphantly its creation of a mode of thought, a metaphysic of its own, a relationship between the individual and the universe which belongs to no other art, science or philosophy.[1]

THE TYGER

Tyger! Tyger! burning bright
In the forests of the night,
What immortal hand or eye
Could frame thy fearful symmetry?

In what distant deeps or skies
Burnt the fire of thine eyes?
On what wings dare he aspire?
What the hand dare seize the fire?

And what shoulder, and what art,
Could twist the sinews of thy heart?
And when thy heart began to beat,
What dread hand? and what dread feet?

What the hammer? what the chain?
In what furnace was thy brain?
What the anvil? what dread grasp
Dare its deadly terrors clasp?

When the stars threw down their spears,
And water'd heaven with their tears,
Did he smile his work to see?
Did he who made the Lamb make thee?

Tyger! Tyger! burning bright
In the forests of the night,
What immortal hand or eye
Dare frame thy fearful symmetry?

---

[1] See *Countries of the Mind—Series II*. The Metaphysic of Poetry. ￼
Middleton Murry.

How does Blake use imagery in this masterpiece to win his unique effects? What does he create with it, and how does he create it?

First of all, what is he saying? He is posing the eternal question of the problem of evil. Why has brute force and cruelty, beauty? Is it God who created it? If so, does he delight in it? But Blake's method of presenting this theme bears no relation to the philosophical method. The place of abstract speculation of the reasoning faculty is filled by that of concrete suggestion and revelation, that of argument by poetic imagery. At once we are transported to another world, the world of his vision, where he fashions a symbol of the qualities of force and cruelty. It is not an actual flesh and blood tiger we see before us, it is a tiger which evokes at the same time a physical outline and an idea, a blending of the abstract and the concrete, of the body and of the spirit of burning and brightness, of forests and night. Then the creation of the ruthless and exquisite creature is bodied forth in a series of further images where again the physical and the spiritual are inextricably blended. As it, and its creator, blaze before us in all their terror and beauty, into the framework of this poetic universe is drawn another image of magnificent audacity. The stars become the symbols of peace and love. Weeping, they question speechlessly the meaning of the presence of such pitiless cruelty. And in two more images, as dramatic as they are simple, the poet challenges the eternal mystery. Can God delight in horror? Did he create both it and gentleness? There is no structure of intellectual argument: the logic proceeds step by step, implicit in the structure of thought and emotion and sensation awakened by the series of images. And it is this which is the root and foundation of the difference between poetic thought and logical reasoning. Poetry apprehends experience and communicates experience in a fashion entirely its own.

By metaphor the poet can fuse the physical, the emotional and the intellectual worlds into one complex, complete and immediate act of apprehension. And it is that synthesis which is the living heart of poetry.

WORDS

1.

No doubt the time will come when psychology will tell us exactly what does happen within our consciousness when a certain collection of words seizes upon us and sends a dazzle of glory rushing through our veins; or a haunting sweetness ringing in our ears; or brings a shock of surprised delight to our eyes; or kindles a glowing warmth about the heart; or brings us tears. At present we only know that when we read

> Lift up your heads, O ye gates, and be ye lift up, ye everlasting doors: and the King of Glory shall come in.

or

> The horns of Elfland faintly blowing.

or

> And hearken to the birds' love-learned song
> The dewy leaves among.

or

> And mighty poets in their misery dead.

or

> Everyone suddenly burst out singing.

or

> He is dead and gone, lady,

a certain sense of enchantment fastens upon many of us. Not, of course, upon everyone. There is always the examinee who paraphrased

> Heard melodies are sweet, but those unheard
> Are sweeter;

as 'it is nice to listen to music, but it is nicer not to'. But for anyone who possesses the 'sense of words', which is the same thing as the sense of poetry, a certain leaping of attention takes place, a brightening of the inward eye, a flame of response.

We are accustomed to speak of such lines of poetry as 'magical', and indeed they do bring a revelation with them. But it is not a revelation of anything supernatural, but a revelation of the natural power lying prisoned in words; a power which the poet can release. R. L. Stevenson, writing about style, makes an extraordinary statement about language. 'The sister arts,' he says, 'enjoy the use of a plastic and ductile material, like the modeller's clay; literature alone is condemned to work in mosaic with finite and quite rigid words.' Finite and rigid seem odd epithets for a conscious stylist to apply to words. For words are not mere collections of letters of the alphabet, with a finite meaning and a rigid shape: nor are they mere audible syllables of loveliness or ugliness. They are the storehouse of innumerable traditional and individual associations, which awaken to life at their sight and sound, and which give them their beauty and their power. And it is because of this power in words that the emotional experiences of poetry, although they can never be as acute as those of actual living, are possessed of far greater resonance and reverberation.

There are certain words which are inseparable from the idea of poetry. We cannot think of the nightingale or the rose, of love or sleep or death, of the moon and the sea, of the hills and the wind, of gold and silver, of

woods and wild flowers, without a rush of poetic emo-
tion and poetic colouring. *The horns of Elfland faintly
blowing,* besides all the melody of its liquid and labial
letters, is haunted with all the mystery of faeryland and
all the adventure of the chase—remote, half-heard, and
mingled together to create an effect as enchanting as it is
imponderable. *And mighty poets in their misery dead*
conveys all that can be evoked of nobility, grandeur and
beauty by the words 'mighty poets', with all that is
added to them and changed in them by the juxtaposi-
tion of the full body of the words 'misery' and 'dead':
all the burden of the mystery, the weary weight of all
the unintelligible world. Those four words associated to-
gether, set up reverberations in the human spirit which
echo to the confines of man's thought.

2.

POETRY is words. It is a certain way of using words, so
that they take on a vitality which they have in no other
use of them. Every significance which words can carry
in speech or prose is intensified in poetry—quality of
sound, shades of meaning, symbolic importance—but as
well as this sharpening of value, there is a creation of
new values, which belong to the poetic use of words
alone. They work with a secret potency, they take on
a new personality. They may not be distinguished or
unusual at all, indeed they can be of the barest sim-
plicity:

> Thou'll break my heart, thou bonnie bird,
>   That sings upon the bough;
> Thou minds me o' the happy days
>   When my fause Luve was true.

But their choice and ordering seem inevitable, they
create a harmony, a security, a conviction.

It is neither the width of a poet's vocabulary, nor the particular character of that vocabulary which gives it value. It is true that Shakespeare has a larger range of words than anyone else, but it is the quality of his use of them and not the quantity at his disposal which make him the greatest of poets, just as it is the quality of his creation of emotion, and not the number of human types he brings upon the stage, which make him the greatest of dramatists. For the poet is concerned with language *as a means to an end*, and it is in the degree in which he has achieved that end that he must be judged. He may wish to group the intellectual and emotional and physical symbols, which are his material, as if they were flowers arranged in a little formal Victorian bouquet in a paper frill: he may wish to give them the appearance of the happy richness of a chance arrangement in a pottery pitcher: or he may aim at the subtle and complex adaptation and emphasis of a Japanese bowl. The single flowers, his words, will be from the common stock, but their values at once become different according to their environment, and require a different critical adjustment in the reader.

The lesser poet, or the great poet when he is writing as a less great one, uses the surface of words only. He can create most beautiful effects with them out of sound and pattern and colour combinations and the simple emotional responses, such as the marvellous verbal felicities of Tennyson, for example, or Herrick's delicious grace and daintiness. And he asks from the reader only what he has demanded of the words himself. But the finer the poet, the fuller and richer will be the value of his words and the necessary response of the reader. It is not only their surface, but their whole content and substance which has to be savoured: their sound in the ear and their taste and feel in the mouth; a sense of their plasticity and density; their colouring from the past;

their echoes and associations; their disposal and manipulation in the poem itself, and all the modifications of their significance which arise from that. It is amazing how a single word can make a whole poem by an isolation of it in a special use which brings a throb of unexpected discovery, a sudden realization of feeling and seeing it in the mind. Compare the use of the word 'roves' for instance in the following verses. The first is from Dr. Johnson's *Ode to Spring*,

> Now o'er the rural Kingdom roves
> Soft pleasure with her laughing train;
> Love warbles in the vocal groves
> And vegetation plants the plain.

The second is from Walter de la Mare:

> Very old are the woods;
>   And the buds that break
> Out of the briar's boughs,
>   When March winds wake,
> So old with their beauty are
>   Oh, no man knows
> Through what wild centuries
>   Roves back the rose.

3.

As in every division of poetic technique, there are both unconscious and conscious elements to be considered in the poet's use of words: the elements which spring from personality and those which are the result of craftsmanship. There are certain poets whose personalities are so individual that their peculiar vocabularies are an inseparable part of their total effect. No one but Milton could have written:

> Of Abana and Pharphar, lucid streams,

just as no one but Hopkins could have written

> Towery city and branchy between towers,

and no one but Browning

What of soul was left, I wonder, when the kissing had to stop?

and no one but Swinburne

> For Winter's rains and ruins are over
> And all the season of snows and sins,

and no one but Eliot

> And bones cast in a little low dry garret,
> Rattled by the rats' foot only, year to year.

If we read the words 'sweet cheat' or 'Beauty vanishes, Beauty passes, however rare, rare, it be', we say 'de la Mare': if we read 'Shoulder the sky, my lad, and drink your ale', we say 'Housman'. We have only to imagine well-known poems transposed into another key of diction to realize just how typical of their authors are certain uses of language. J. C. Squire illustrated some years ago what might happen in such a case. Among other light-hearted suggestions, he imagined Pope writing Tennyson's *Break, break, break* . . . when the two middle verses became

> See how the labour of the urgent oar
> Propels the barks and draws them to the shore.
> Hark! from the margin of the azure bay
> The joyful cries of infants at their play.
> (The offspring of a piscatorial swain,
> His home the sands, his pasturage the main.)
> Yet none of these may soothe the mourning heart,
> Nor fond alleviation's sweets impart;
> Nor may the pow'rs of infants that rejoice
> Restore the accents of a former voice,
> Nor the bright smiles of ocean's nymphs command
> The pleasing contact of a vanished hand.

And Collins did the same thing in all seriousness when
he translated

> with fairest flowers
> While summer lasts and I live here, Fidele,
> I'll sweeten thy sad grave

into:

> To fair Fidele's grassy tomb
> Soft maids and village hinds shall bring
> Each opening sweet of earliest bloom
> And rifle all the breathing spring.

As with individuals, so with the times in which they
live. It is usual to give the name 'poetic diction' to a
peculiarly artificial use of words popular in the eight-
eenth century, when a breeze was always a zephyr; a girl
a nymph; women 'the fair'; fishes, birds and sheep, the
finny prey, the feathered choir and the fleecy care; and
rats, the whiskered vermin race. We cannot conceive by
any stretch of imagination of Rupert Brooke calling fish
the finny prey, or of D. H. Lawrence referring to
women as 'the fair', or of T. S. Eliot calling his rats the
whiskered vermin race. But it was not the eighteenth
century only which evolved a 'poetic diction'. The Eliza-
bethan fondness for hair like gold wires, for hey nonny
noes and for bombasting out blank verse; the Victorian
taste for fine sounding abstractions, and for clipping
prepositions into i', o', wi', o'er and so on, and the 'mod-
ernist' self-conscious avoidance of *any* traditional poetic
vocabulary, are all part of the same thing. Ages have
personalities as well as individuals, and both express
themselves in peculiarities of vocabulary. It is one of the
great technical difficulties of the poet that his art differs
from music in not having a keyboard that is constant.
Words change their value with age and use: sometimes
becoming more exquisite with the patina of the cen-
turies, sometimes becoming sterile and overworked like

land. Figurative language especially loses its force. The
conventional cliché was once a freshly coined image, and
language which seems strained and strange in one age
becomes commonplace to the next. Language, says
Emerson, is fossil poetry. What must Shakespeare have
sounded like to an Elizabethan audience, for instance,
when the words *savage, numerous, obscure, conscious,
jovial, damp, clumsy, clutched, strenuous* had all been
attacked by purists as new-fangled? He himself made
the first use of *assassination, bare-faced, bump, count-
less, critic, disgraceful, dwindle, fitful, gloomy, heart-
sore, ill-starred, impartial, lonely, monumental, sportive,*
and a host of others. We cannot, naturally, imagine those
words carrying an atmosphere of challenge and experi-
ment, and to read or hear Shakespeare with the ears of
an Elizabethan would be a completely new experience.
It is even impossible for us to-day to gauge at all ade-
quately the shock of *Lyrical Ballads* to the taste of its
age, and the radical readjustment necessary to the origi-
nal readers.

4.

ALTHOUGH the term 'poetic diction' is itself a term
which use has staled, and which carries with it connota-
tions of the artificial and the empty, the problem of
poetic diction in the simple sense of the word is the
poet's gravest concern. Nature will inevitably endow
him with certain inescapable characteristics in his use of
words. He will be thrifty like Housman or Hardy, or
spendthrift like Marlowe or Swinburne; cool like Col-
lins or boisterous like Browning; bluff like Chesterton
or exquisite like de la Mare; urban like Dryden or coun-
trified like Clare. He will instinctively reach first after
perfection of line and movement, like Wordsworth or
Marvell, or first after richness of suggestion in language,
like Yeats or Shelley. But whatever may be the uncon-

scious bias of his personality towards certain values, the whole conscious force of his artistry will be towards the most exact precision he can attain between the words he uses and the effect he wishes to communicate. He will be driven remorselessly by the spirit within him until that spirit has embodied itself in its verbal equivalent, until it has a local habitation and a *name*. This quest is at once his torture and his joy. 'I know not how to express my devotion,' writes Keats to Fanny Brawne, 'I want a brighter word than bright, a fairer word than fair.' Or, as a modern poet, Clere Parsons, prays,

> Mallarmé for a favour
> teach me to achieve
> the rigid gesture won only with labour
> and comparable to the ease
> balance and strength with which the ballet-dancer
> sustains her still mercurial pose in air.

A study of a poet's own corrections often brings home vividly the labour which preceded the final perfect achievement. Milton's 'airy tongues that syllable men's names' was first the commonplace 'airy tongues that lure night wanderers'; and the exquisite veracity of Keats's

> Not so much life as on a summer's day
> Robs not one light seed from the feathered grass

might have remained

> Not so much life as on a summer's day
> Robs not at all the dandelion's fleece.

The poet may use words for their own sakes, or for what they bring with them, for their sound or their sense—or both. The first use is a very small one, and applies really only to refrains which are intentionally meaningless. But the poet frequently orchestrates his language so that the reader is expected to pay next to no attention to anything but the sensuous and emotional value of the sound pattern. It is the actual syllabic texture of the words he is to live in: if he surrender himself to that, slicing off only the thinnest surface of their 'meaning', they will bring all that is needful for a just interpretation. An extreme illustration can be taken from Vachel Lindsay's *The Congo*:

> Fat black bucks in a wine-barrel room,
> Barrel house kings, with feet unstable,
> Sagged and reeled and pounded on the table,
> Pounded on the table,
> Beat an empty barrel with the handle of a broom
> Hard as they were able,
> Boom, boom BOOM
> With a silk umbrella and the handle of a broom
> Boomlay, boomlay, boomlay, BOOM.

As a contrast in effect, see how the hard consonants and short clipped vowels, all the energetic jerkiness of the rhythm in this verse of Browning, conveys the parallel of active vigorous moral effort:

> Then welcome each rebuff
> That turns earth's smoothness rough,
> Each sting that bids nor sit nor stand but go!
> Be our joys three-parts pain!
> Strive, and hold cheap the strain;
> Learn, nor account the pang; dare, never grudge the throe!

Or, as another contrast, this stanza from Ben Jonson:

> Have you seen but a bright lily grow
>   Before rude hands have touch'd it?
> Have you mark'd but the fall of the snow
>   Before the soil hath smutch'd it?
> Have you felt the wool of beaver,
>   Or swan's down ever?
> Or have smelt o' the bud o' the brier,
>   Or the nard in the fire?

Or have tasted the bag of the bee?
O so white, O so soft, O so sweet is she!

In this last example, sight shares with sound the impressions evoked by the words, and it is typical of all the poetry where the poet asks us to experience sensation only, to respond with the senses, with ear and eye and touch and taste and smell, as vividly and keenly as may be. Rupert Brooke's *The Great Lover* is a good example of such poetry, or a concentrated example is this stanza from *St. Agnes' Eve:*

> And still she slept an azure-lidded sleep,
> In blanchèd linen, smooth and lavender'd,
> While he from forth the closet brought a heap
> Of candied apple, quince and plum, and gourd;
> With jellies soother than the creamy curd
> And lucent syrops tinct with cinnamon;
> Manna and dates in argosy transferr'd
> From Fez; and spiced dainties every one,
> From silken Samarcand to cedar'd Lebanon.

But the most interesting poetry for the study of the use of language is where the poet is consciously working with as rich and pregnant a sense of word value as he can command. Against him are ranged all the forces of custom. His readers have eyes blurred with the film of familiarity and ears muffled by common usage; minds grooved with habit and stiff with convention. He has to bring them eyes and ears and hearts, to 'stab the spirit broad awake' with words. And he has no preparation of the reader's mind to help him—no medium such as paint or instrument or stage, to gain attention at the start. Only such stimulus and attentiveness which springs from the sight of irregular lines on the printed page. And the medium of communication itself is only a different use of the same medium with which his audience carry on all their communication with their fellows—the currency of language: debased, defaced and worn. Yet by rhythm and melody, by the intellectual, emotional and physical vibrations which he can at once set up, he can create the whole 'feel' of a poem by the choice and placing of the words in the first lines. For the quality of words arranged in verse forms influence and modify each other, like colour values in painting, and work in a flash upon the mind in the most subtle and unexplained fashion.

> White in the moon the long road lies
> The moon stands blank above;

At once we are prepared for the conclusion:

> White in the moon the long road lies
> That leads me from my love.

If the last line ran 'that leads me *to* my love', the opening, though equally true to fact, would be poetically false, for the feeling has already been created by the association of the words 'white', 'long' and 'blank'. It is already there: all the weariness and forlornness and emptiness and chill, and our minds are focussed to that mood. Equally the whole effect can be ruined by the wrong word. It is useless for Burns to prepare us for a beautiful lament by writing

> Ae fond kiss, and then we sever!
> Ae fareweel, and then for ever!

if he writes in the next verse,

> I'll ne'er blame my partial fancy,
> Naething could resist my Nancy.

The mood is at once irrevocably shattered.

Perhaps the most obvious way in which the poet pricks the reader's attention to life is by his use of epithets. Epithets, indeed, can be revelations. Revelations of immediate concrete satisfactions such as 'meadows *trim* with daisies *pied*', or 'the *rough male* kiss of blankets', or 'the windflower *chilly*, with all the winds at play', or

> *Frail* brother of the morn,
> That from the *tiny* bents and *misted* leaves
> Withdraws his *timid* horn,
> And *fearful* vision weaves.

or

> And ghastly through the drizzling rain
> On the *bald* street breaks the *blank* day.

or '*smock-faced* sheep', or the '*twelve-winded* sky', or 'the tiger moth's *deep-damasked* wings'. Here, in the one word *damask* is concentrated the ideas of the sheen and texture of silk and metal and roses—just as T. S. Eliot's creation of the name of the Princess *Volupine* telescopes the idea of voluptuousness with that of the carcase-devouring of the vulture and the slyness of the fox.

Or epithets may be revelations by using familiar words in an unexpected way:

'I taught my silks their *whistling* to forbear.' Or by blending the abstract and the concrete so that each gains a new force: 'the *same, bright, patient* stars', '*proud pied* April', 'the *lazy leaden-stepping* hours'. Or again by setting the heart vibrating by a new grouping of words it has heard a thousand times: '*Old, unhappy, far-off* things', 'Ladies *dead* and *lovely* knights', or

> And there shall be for thee all *soft* delight
> That *shadowy* thought can win;
> A *bright* torch and a casement ope at night
> To let the *warm* Love in.

5.

IT is impossible to say where the line between words which can and words which cannot be used in poetry, comes. Indeed, there is no such line. Wordsworth said that anything was material for poetry which could be brought into manifest and palpable relation with us as enjoying and suffering beings, and perhaps the same is true of words. The handicap which the poet incurs by making use of scientific terms, of slang, or of obscure allusions is that the language is necessarily impoverished of emotional associations and the emotional associations evoked by words are their richest value to the poet. When a poet writes

> Shall we
> Insulate our strong currents of ecstasy
> Or breed units of power?

there is none of the instinctive stirring of the heart which is brought to us all by the old familiar symbols of fertility and fecundity; Ceres, the flowers and fruits of the earth, love, springtime. The words are emotionally sterile. Similarly with the use of allusions. Allusions do not in themselves make a poet intellectual, any more than baggage covered with foreign hotel labels makes a man cosmopolitan, but they serve a very real purpose in poetry. Through their use, the poet can employ a species of shorthand, he can compare and contrast the whole atmosphere of his own experience with the whole atmosphere of that of others by a sudden quotation or echo which releases the memory of his reader and sets it in a prepared channel. But the necessary response must be there waiting to be released, and if it is not, again the poet's words remain sterile. This is what makes so much of T. S. Eliot empty of content to the average reader. Though he may make use of words in themselves full of

poetic suggestions, they frequently fail completely to
carry the associations which the poet expects of them.
When he writes:

> To Carthage then I came

> Burning, burning, burning, burning
> O Lord Thou pluckest me out
> O Lord Thou pluckest

> burning

the average reader receives nothing at all. Even when he
has learnt that 'To Carthage then I came' is a quotation
from St. Augustine, and 'burning, burning, burning,
burning' a quotation from Buddha's Fire Sermon, and
that the collocation of the two suggest the two great
types of eastern and western asceticism, it is as likely as
not that the suggestion will refuse stubbornly to come.
The poet is demanding of the words more than they can
perform. Although actually, as words, 'Carthage', 'pluck-
est' and 'burning' are full of memory and suggestion,
their use here has no poetry in them, for their order and
grouping do not direct the reader's response into any
channel where they mingle harmoniously; where they
co-ordinate.

And just as words seemingly proper to poetry may
fail of their value, so, in spite of Dr. Johnson's declara-
tion that every man perceives himself irresistibly alien-
ated by low terms, the most colloquial language can
find a place in poetry if it is handled by a master. For
words in poetry can be chameleons. They can take on
different colours from their environment and company,
and it is possible to subdue the most apparently intrac-
table syllables to a general harmony from which one
would imagine they would stand out like a jazz melody
in a Bach Mass.

But there is no point on which readers differ more than on this. Just as Donne's image of the compasses repels certain minds, so does, for instance, Browning's use of the word 'scratch' in *Meeting at Night*:

> The gray sea and the long black land;
> And the yellow half-moon large and low;
> And the startled little waves that leap
> In fiery ringlets from their sleep,
> As I gain the cove with pushing prow,
> And quench its speed i' the slushy sand.
>
> Then a mile of warm sea-scented beach;
> Three fields to cross till a farm appears;
> A tap at the pane, the quick sharp scratch
> And blue spurt of a lighted match,
> And a voice less loud, thro' its joys and fears,
> Than the two hearts beating each to each.

One American critic writes of this that no one would seriously contend that *the quick sharp scratch and blue spurt of a lighted match* is anything more than excellent prose. 'Its effect is complete with the mere sensory visualisation. It provokes no reaction in our nerve centers that we identify as emotion.' Whereas to anyone who is caught up in the atmosphere of leaping eagerness and fire and fear which moulds the whole organic rhythm of that poem, the words, as used by the poet *in that context*, seem an inseparable part of the quality of the experience and communicate in sound and colour and movement the precise emotional vitality of that moment.

Or take the poem, *I say, I'll seek her*, by Thomas Hardy.

> I say, "I'll seek her side
> Ere hindrance interposes;"
> But eve in midnight closes
> And here I still abide.

When darkness wears I see
Her sad eyes in a vision;
They ask, "What indecision
Detains you, Love, from me?

"The creaking hinge is oiled,
I have unbarred the backway,
But you tread not the trackway;
And shall the thing be spoiled?

"Far cockcrows echo shrill,
The shadows are abating
And I am waiting, waiting;
But O, you tarry still!"

Here the shift of tone which the words *backway* and
trackway and the conversational *and shall the thing be
spoiled?* bring, in no way jar the sensitive reader. They
add a world of concrete reality to the abstract presences
of darkness and indecision and waiting; giving a human
solidity to the emotional situation, particularizing the
vagueness created by the traditional poetic vocabulary—
eve, abide, vision, abating, tarry—into a clear firm out-
line.

Another example where opinions may differ as to the
success of a verbal boldness is in a famous sonnet of
Donne.

At the round earth's imagin'd corners blow
Your trumpets, angels, and arise, arise
From death, you numberless infinities
Of souls, and to your scattered bodies go;
All whom the flood did, and fire shall o'erthrow,
All whom war, dearth, age, agues, tyrannies,
Despair, law, chance hath slain, and you, whose eyes
Shall behold God, and never taste death's woe.

But let them sleep, Lord, and me mourn a space;
For, if above all these my sins abound,
'Tis late to ask abundance of Thy grace,
When we are there. Here on this lowly ground,
Teach me how to repent, for that's as good
As if Thou hadst seal'd my pardon with Thy blood.

Does the sudden drop to colloquialisms in *that's as good*
bring something of value into the poem, as it does in the
Hardy lyric; or is it a mere discordant check to the
splendour? Does it sharpen the emotion, or is the mood
bruised and bent?

THE CONTINUITY OF POETRY

I.

Not on sad Stygian shore, nor in clear sheen
Of far Elysian plain, shall we meet those
Among the dead whose pupils we have been,
Nor those great shades whom we have held as foes;
No meadow of asphodel our feet shall tread,
Nor shall we look each other in the face
To love or hate each other being dead,
Hoping some praise, or fearing some disgrace.
We shall not argue, saying " 'Twas thus," or "thus,"
Our argument's whole drift we shall forget;
Who's right, who's wrong, 'twill be all one to us;
We shall not even know that we have met.
    Yet meet we shall, and part, and meet again,
    Where dead men meet, on lips of living men.

                (Samuel Butler)

WE have now seen something of the rhythms and patterns which the poet's use of words builds up in his poem, and we have seen how those rhythms not only harmonize and co-ordinate and unify the material of the poet's experience, but also communicate themselves to the reader, harmonizing and co-ordinating his responses, and thus enriching and invigorating his whole being. But there is another aspect of the effect of poetry, which we have not yet discussed and which in one way is the largest aspect of all. It, also, is based on the idea of the harmony of parts which form a whole—that conception which seems to be behind every large satisfaction of the human consciousness, and which has made humanity seek so patiently and passionately 'how many ways and days', to find some principle of harmony in the universe at large; to conceive of, and to believe in, some scheme in which man plays a part in a universal system and co-ordination. Poetry can create for many sensitive readers an illusion, at least, of such a harmony: in it they can feel that its profound organic rhythms are an echo of a universal rhythm, hidden from their apprehension, but definitely *there*. Hence all the vague transcendental terms which critics have employed all down the ages to try and convey their sense of this assurance.

But whether or not we can share in the conviction of that cosmic harmony, there is a more particular sense of unity in space and time which the reading of much poetry inevitably creates. 'The Poet,' says Wordsworth, 'binds together by passion and knowledge the vast empire of human society as it is spread over the whole earth and over all time.' When we read the book of Job or the plays of Euripides, *Samson Agonistes* or *King Lear,* we listen to different tones of the same human voice crying in its agony 'God of our Fathers, what is Man?' When we read the Song of Solomon or a lyric of Li Po, an ode of Horace or a sonnet of Petrarch, a song of Burns or a poem of Walter de la Mare, we hear the 'linkèd sweetness long drawn out' of the moments of life and love which were the same three thousand years ago as they are today. In poetry, suddenly, across the ages, we catch the veritable accents of innumerable generations of men and women, whose actual daily speech has passed away without leaving so much as a trace of its existence.

Even in English and American poetry, which is all we can concern ourselves with here, that sense of unity with our past springs to life as we read. Suddenly comes the realization that types of personality are eternal, and that whatever age they live in, these types will produce the same kind of poetry, however different it may be in degree. The creative, character-making type will produce now a Chaucer, now a Shakespeare, now a Browning; the conscious artist is now a Pope, now a Rossetti, now a Housman; the solitary mystic appears as a Vaughan, as a Blake, as an Emily Brontë; the sophisticated man of the world writes in one age as a Dryden, in another as a Byron; the intellectual takes one incarnation in a Donne and another in a Shelley and another in an Eliot; the great struggle between the Puritan and the Epicurean fights itself out in one age in the splendour of a Milton, in another in the unhappiness of an Arnold.

And as with individual types, so with the themes of which they write. There is no common human emotion which is ever out of date, for though the emotions may be attached to ways of thought and schemes of belief in which we have no part, the human needs which call them forth remain the same. It may be the joy of youth and love:

> In a harbour grene aslepe whereas I lay,
> The byrdes sang swete in the middes of the day,
> I dreamed fast of mirth and play:
>   In youth is pleasure, in youth is pleasure.

Or the joy of returned vitality after an eclipse of spirits:

> And now in age I bud again,
> After so many deaths I live and write;
> I once more smell the dew and rain,
> And relish versing: O my only light,
>   It cannot be
>   That I am he
> On whom thy tempests fell all night.

Or the cry of overstrained faith:

> Wert thou mine enemy, O thou my friend,
> How would'st thou worse, I wonder, than thou dost
> Defeat, thwart me?

Or a burst of vigorous courage:

> Out of the night that covers me,
> Black as the pit from pole to pole,
> I thank whatever gods may be
> For my unconquerable soul.

Or the complete rapture and agony of the mystic experience and its passing:

> But first, a hush of peace—a soundless calm descends;
> The struggle of distress and fierce impatience ends.
> Mute music soothes my breast—unutter'd harmony
> That I could never dream, till Earth was lost to me.
>
> Then dawns the Invisible; the Unseen its truth reveals;
> My outward sense is gone, my inward essence feels;
> Its wings are almost free—its home, its harbour found;
> Measuring the gulf, it stoops, and dares the final bound.
>
> O dreadful is the check—intense the agony—
> When the ear begins to hear, and the eye begins to see;
> When the pulse begins to throb—the brain to think again—
> The soul to feel the flesh, and the flesh to feel the chain.

Or the dear memory of old love:

> How sad and bad and mad it was—
> But then, how it was sweet!

Or the heartache which is behind experience:

> Ah, love, let us be true
> To one another! for the world, which seems
> To lie before us like a land of dreams,
> So various, so beautiful, so new,

Hath really neither joy, nor love, nor light,
Nor certitude, nor peace, nor help for pain;
And we are here as on a darkling plain
Swept with confused alarms of struggles and flight,
Where ignorant armies clash by night.

2.

THE unity of the great world of poetry, like the
unity of any individual consciousness, is the fusion of
many parts to form a whole. The elements of poetry are
the same from everlasting to everlasting. Men and
women all down the ages have faced the same eternal
human problems, have asked the same eternal human
questions, and have suffered and enjoyed the same eter-
nal human emotions. In age after age those men and
women who have possessed what we call the poetic vision
have striven to find patterned words for what they have
seen and heard and felt and thought of human life. But
the colouring and flavour each has unconsciously given
to his poetry by creating it in the terms of his own
times and his own temperament, introduces so many
modifications and unlikenesses that it is sometimes diffi-
cult to believe that the elements are still essentially the
same, and that it is only the co-ordination of them which
differs. It is as Robert Bridges says in *The Testament of
Beauty:*

                              our moods
    influences and spiritual affections are like
    those many organic substances which, tho' to sense
    wholly dissimilar and incomparable in kind,
    are yet all combinations of the same simples,
    and even in like proportions differently disposed;
    so that whether it be starch, oil, sugar or alcohol
    'tis ever our old customers, carbon and hydrogen,
    pirouetting with oxygen in their morris antics.

Art never improves, says T. S. Eliot. It is only what we call the spirit of the age, and the personality of the artist, which are the perpetually shifting components in works of art. And indeed in one sense there is no spirit of the age except the spirit of the present age, and no eyes except our own. Through them we see and judge all, and the past is re-adjusted according to the quality of vision possessed by the present: it is altered by the present as much as the present has been shaped by the past. 'There is no catholicity of taste which will equip a man to appreciate ways of thought that are fundamentally hostile and mutually exclusive.' We can imagine the spirit of our age as a fixed beam of light and the complete human consciousness as a many faceted surface, all of which facets cannot be lighted at one time from the same source. Inevitably we miss what other ages may have seen, just as we see what other ages have inevitably missed. At one and the same time we are clear-sighted and we are blind.

For purposes of criticism, however, it is easier to speak of the spirit of past ages as if they really possessed the objective reality they appear to us to have, and we shall continue so to speak of them. But there is a further point to remember here, and that is that what we are accustomed to regard as the spirit of an age in the past, is very frequently the spirit of a poet, or poets, who, when they were writing, were in conscious revolt from their age. As I. A. Richards says: 'the poet is the point at which the growth of the mind shows itself.' Poets such as Chaucer, or Donne, or Dryden, or Wordsworth and Coleridge, by the force of their individual vision and creative power, appear to change the whole current of literature. So it is over and over again in the history of art. The great poet revolts from the past, and re-creates the elements of life and thought into fresh organic structures. It is not that the material of his experience is any different from that of his age in general, but the *way* he experiences it—the 'style' he gives it—these make of it a new thing. Then, when the poet has become 'recognized' by the age, which means that the age has recognized itself in the poet, and that 'point' at which the growth of the mind has showed itself has become generalized, then in a flood comes 'the spirit of the age'. All the imitable qualities in the poet's matter and manner rapidly become a fashion, and remain so until again a new vision and a new synthesis happen. It is not until the whole movement belongs sufficiently to the past to be seen in just perspective that we are alive to it. For as Donne said of his portrait, so it is true of a poet and his poetry:

> 'Tis like me now, but I dead, 'twill be more
> When we are shadows both, than 'twas before.

3.

WHAT then is the course of our own literary history? Whence did it come and where is it now and whither is it going? How have individuals and public opinion interplayed within it? What different facets of man's consciousness have been illumined by it? In what perspectives have the elements of poetry arranged themselves: what syntheses have been achieved: what harmony results? Here is matter for many more books, but perhaps we can see enough of the past to feel its essential unity with the present.

Modern man in England emerges at the Renaissance. Even Chaucer, with his sanity and his humour, his pity and his tolerance, his keenness of external observation and his flashes of insight, lacks something. His attitude is one of acceptance of life as it is:

What is this world? What asketh men to have?
Now with his love, now in his colde grave
Allone, with-outen any companye.
Thanne is it wisdom, as it thinketh me,
To maken vertu of necessitee,
And take it wel.

And we can perhaps illustrate best what it is that
Chaucer lacks, by a quotation from an Elizabethan poet
—Sir John Davies.

I know my body's of so frail a kind
    As force without, fevers within, can kill;
I know the heavenly nature of my mind,
    But 'tis corrupted both in wit and will;

I know my soul hath power to know all things,
    Yet is she blind and ignorant in all;
I know I am one of nature's little kings,
    Yet to the least and vilest thing am thrall.

I know my life's a pain and but a span,
    I know my sense is mocked in everything;
And to conclude, I know myself a man,
    Which is a proud, and yet a wretched thing.

It is the note of challenge to life that is lacking in
medieval literature; the knowledge of the freedom of
the individual to explore the mystery of its own being.
The Renaissance saw the birth of the critical and analyti-
cal mind, and hence the birth of the poetry of personal
relationships. The poets no longer write of man in rela-
tion to a fixed scheme of cosmic, religious or chivalrous
values, they write of the direct experiences of individual
men in relation to God, to nature, to knowledge, to each
other, to women. And this analytical spirit, young and
experimental in Spenser and the sonneteers, and matur-
ing gradually in the great dramatic movement of the

age, comes to its complete point of self-consciousness in John Donne (1573-1631). Donne, like Bacon, took all knowledge for his province, but he has little interest in knowledge as such. He is a great poet—that is, he brings all he has learnt and read and thought into direct kinship with his emotional experience. His love of woman, and later his love of God, is knit up with the whole of his apprehension of the sensuous and intellectual worlds. It is one with all the elements of the physical universe, with all the professional terminology of the court, of the law, of the church, of trade, of the sciences: with cynicism and with ecstasy, with lust and with mystical passion, with anger, fear, jealousy, disgust, and with perfect peace.

THE SUN RISING

Busy old fool, unruly sun,
   Why dost thou thus,
Through windows and through curtains call on us?
Must to thy motions lovers seasons run?
   Saucy pedantic wretch, go chide
   Late school-boys, and sour prentices,
Go tell Court-huntsmen, that the King will ride,
Call country ants to harvest offices;
Love, all alike, no season knows, nor clime,
Nor hours, days, months, which are the rags of time.

Thy beams, so reverend and strong
   Why shouldst thou think?
I could eclipse and cloud them with a wink,
But that I would not lose her sight so long:
   If her eyes have not blinded thine,
   Look, and tomorrow late, tell me,
Whether both the Indias, of spice and mine,
Be where thou leftst them, or lie here with me.
Ask for those Kings whom thou saw'st yesterday,
And thou shalt hear, All here in one bed lay.

> She is all States, and all Princes, I,
>   Nothing else is.
> Princes do but play us; compar'd to this
> All honour's mimic; All wealth alchemy.
>   Thou sun art half as happy as we,
>   In that the world's contracted thus;
>   Thine age asks ease, and since thy duties be
>   To warm the world, that's done in warming us.
> Shine here to us, and thou art everywhere;
> This bed thy centre is, these walls, thy sphere.

For a generation after Donne's death almost every minor poet wrote like Donne. Sophisticated love poetry and intimately personal religious poetry were the two popular channels of expression, and although of course the personality of each poet colours his work—and the age of Herrick and Herbert, Vaughan and Marvell, Carew and Lovelace, is an age of great charm and originality of personality—yet through them all persist those qualities in Donne which could be imitated; the fashion of using esoteric images, and of combining their use with a colloquial use of language, in which speech rhythms were blended with those of the written word. Then, while Milton was creating new organic rhythms of thought and words in the loneliness of supreme genius, the reaction against the 'metaphysicals' came from another quarter. The new king (Charles II) and his court brought back all the new French ideals of writing from his exile—the ideals of clarity and directness of presentation and 'a close, naked, natural way of speaking' in both verse and prose. Again one man, John Dryden, born in the year that Donne died, imposed a new approach to experience and a new formal technique upon poetry. Its elements appeared to him to have become distorted and disrupted by the artifices of the metaphysical 'conceit':

> Since that the thing we call the world,
> By chance on atoms is begot,
> Which though in daily motions hurl'd
> Yet weary not,
> How doth it prove
> Thou art so fair and I in love?

So sang the metaphysical poet, and was prepared to prove it in any number of complicated ways. Dryden's vision saw a very different world. It was a world mapped and planned by a practical intelligence, by a masculine ideal of sanity and discipline. It rested upon a scheme of thought which accepted certain premises about the nature of God and man, and ordered the rest of the universe accordingly. Its great controlling force was the rational faculty in man's nature, and the great civilizing power of poetry must support and further that force. Just as the social and intellectual forces of the later Renaissance seemed to become incarnated in Donne, so the social and intellectual forces of the Restoration seemed to become incarnate in Dryden. Profound social changes were in the air. The Civil War had been fought and the middle-class had emerged triumphant—a middle-class which represented a huge new potential reading public. Man in general, after all the turmoil and unrest of the war wanted again to become a social animal: he wanted an orderly, stable, safe way of life. He congregated in towns; he became urban and gregarious; he invented the coffee house as a centre for business and culture and gossip; his standards of literature became mundane and bourgeois; 'I hold it very indecent,' said Shaftesbury, in 1711, when Dryden's creation of the new values had again turned into the general fashion of thought of the day, 'I hold it very indecent that a man should publish his meditations or solitary thoughts. Those are the froth and scum of writing, which should be unburdened in private and consigned to oblivion, before the writer comes before the world as good company.' It is not surprising that the popular poetic figure of Shaftesbury's day should be Pope, 'the wicked wasp of Twickenham', the most brilliant purveyor of social gossip who has ever written verse, and whose wit and point and lucidity and exquisite precision of statement made him the perfect artist for the age whose ideal of a writer was that he should be 'good company'.

But as was again natural, behind this fashion of urban and common-sense poetry, the forces were gestating which were to embody themselves in the great figures of Wordsworth and Coleridge, and afterwards to decline gradually into the general fashion for romantic verse of the middle and late Victorian Age.

The new creation of poetic values, while it was in complete revolt from the eighteenth century ideal, was again different from that of the Renaissance and of Donne, and to our modern eyes, not only different, but definitely inferior. Great poetry, as we have said, depends on the association of the whole man with the material of his poem. The poet is neither an intellectual nor an emotional being alone; he feels his thoughts and thinks his sensations as it were. If only a part of him is involved in the creation of his symbols—only his senses or only his intellect or only his emotions—his poetry will fail of being great poetry. And the failure of nineteenth century poetry, when it does fail, is precisely in this narrowing of the responses of the poet. When Wordsworth is a great poet, when he is writing the Lucy poems or *The Solitary Reaper,* when Coleridge creates *The Ancient Mariner,* when Keats writes anything, almost, when Shelley writes the *Ode to the West Wind,* when Tennyson writes *Break, break, break,* or Browning *Meeting at Night,* they are great poets. When they are not writing these poems and some others like them, their response to their material tends to lose that fusion of all the activities within them, and to become limited to the reflective and moralizing activity they possess. Instead of being analytical they become ruminative. As T. S. Eliot says, 'the possible interests of a poet are unlimited; the more intelligent he is the better; the more intelligent he is the more likely that he will have interests: our only condition is that he turn them into poetry, and not merely meditate on them poetically.' Henry King (1592-1669) turns flowers and life and death into poetry.

A CONTEMPLATION UPON FLOWERS

Brave flowers, that I could gallant it like you
And be as little vain,
You come abroad and make a harmless show,
And to your beds of earth again;
You are not proud, you know your birth
For your embroidered garments are from earth.

You do obey your months, and times, but I
Would have it ever spring,
My fate would know no winter, never die
Nor think of such a thing;
Oh that I could my bed of earth but view
And smile, and look as cheerfully as you.

Oh teach me to see death, and not to fear
But rather to take truce;
How often have I seen you at a bier,
And there look fresh and spruce;
You fragrant flowers, then teach me that my breath
Like yours may sweeten and perfume my death.

But when Wordsworth writes:

One impulse from a vernal wood
May teach you more of man,
Of moral evil and of good,
Than all the sages can.

he is meditating on flowers poetically. It is a question of the 'message' of the poem being implicit or explicit; whether the moral nature is fused with the rest of the nature of the poet, or whether it stays outside to give its comment on the material of the poem. It is present as much in *A Contemplation upon Flowers* as in *The Tables Turned,* but one is a beautiful little poem and the other is a sermon in verse. Matthew Arnold, indeed, unconsciously revealed the weakness of the ideals held by himself and his age when he defined poetry as 'criticism of life'. As we saw in the first chapter, poetry and criticism are different functions of the consciousness. Poetry apprehends and creates; it is concerned with seizing the whole nature of an experience: criticism is concerned with drawing conclusions from it, with speculating upon it, with trying to comprehend it, with interpreting it.

> Flower in the crannied wall,
> I pluck you out of the crannies,
> I hold you here, root and all, in my hand,
> Little flower—but *if* I could understand
> What you are, root and all, and all in all,
> I should know what God and man is.

Poetry creates the flower and criticism tries to understand it.

4.

THIS tendency to meditate poetically about life instead of creating poetry, was fostered by a change in the relationship between the poet and his environment, which began in the eighteenth century and has progressed steadily ever since. A poet is a member of the society he lives in, just as everyone else is, and it is common knowledge that the potentialities of the individual develop more easily and harmoniously if he feel himself in step with the modes of life and thought around him; if he is at home in his environment, physical, intellectual and emotional. If the major forces and interests of an age are with the poet he can develop much more fully and freely than if they are against him. In the history of English society during the sixteenth and seventeenth centuries, and up to the middle of the eighteenth century, the major forces and interests at work were national, religious and political. Now these ideals and enthusiasms are those in which the whole of a man can be involved, without repression or limitation, and the ages when they held the field are the ages when poetry flourished in a more general way than it has ever since flourished. There was a definite place for poetry in the interests of the age. The poets drew strength and nourishment from the national atmosphere they breathed; it was stimulating and vital. But Milton is the last great poet whom it fed, and the change can be traced from the time of Dryden. At first the interests themselves remained the same, but the stream ran ever more shallow and narrow compared with the full and spacious Elizabethan spirit. It was clear that with the introduction of more sternly rational values, and with the huge new bourgeois reading public, prose would usurp much of the old popularity of poetry. Real poetic inspiration ran underground, and when it next burst out in great individual figures it found itself in an alien environment. The major forces at work in society were rapidly shifting. Vitality had passed from religious interests, and the direction and character of national and political issues had changed. The main currents were industrial and financial, and as the Victorian age developed, they became more and more centred in the progress of science. Byron belonged enough to the general spirit of his times to use his whole talents in satirizing it, and to lose his life in a bid for a new freedom. Shelley flung his whole self into revolt and attempted to create a counterforce which might overthrow the current standards. But the genius of Wordsworth, Coleridge and Keats found nothing in the common interests of the community which could feed their inspiration, nor has any poet since done so. Tennyson bent his genius to please the taste of his age, but he drew no nourishment from it: rather it impoverished him. Browning, like Walt Whitman, had so much animal vitality, such perfectly functioning glands and nerves, that it was of little moment to him what environment he lived in. But the minor Victorian poets were pure individualists, each working his own vein: engrossed by personal religious experience, like Patmore, or Hopkins, or Christina Rossetti; escaping into a world of experience ruled over by 'that Lady Beauty', worshipped by Rossetti or Swinburne; or musing sadly in a cultivated and intelligent way like Arnold or Clough.

The same tendency continued in the new generation of the early twentieth century, but was pushed still further. The domain of poetry had become smaller and smaller. Poetic drama was dead, and the novel had usurped the place of epic and narrative verse. There was still poetry—exquisite poetry very often—written in the old tradition, and an age in which Housman and Hardy and Bridges, Yeats and de la Mare, Robert Frost and Edward Thomas, Edna St. Vincent Millay and Edwin Arlington Robinson were writing can hardly be called a very barren age. But it is nevertheless impossible to read any of these poets today and not to feel that they belong to an age that is passing, and that their rhythms are those of a swan song. Not that there were yet any signs of a new poetry in which the poet identified himself with the spirit of a new civilization. Rather he isolated himself still further, for no longer did he regard himself as the guardian of those spiritual and moral values in life which the growth of the industrial and scientific interests of the world at large were threatening. All the young intellectual bent was towards 'pure poetry', the poetry which, as Gautier said, 'proves nothing and tells nothing'. There was a wave of new interest in the formal 'organization' of Art, but as far as material went the youthful possessor of the poetic vision felt more and more driven in upon himself. His main preoccupation became psychological, the creation of detached moments of experience for their own sakes, unrelated to any social or moral significance. Never before had man been so aware of his own consciousness, or so fascinated by its intricacy.

> To penetrate that room is my desire,
> The extreme attic of the mind, that lies
> Just beyond the last bend in the corridor.

5.

THE 'point' at which the new psychological growth of the mind showed itself was in the poetry of T. S. Eliot. Here we feel a definite impact between a wide and sensitive intelligence and the values of the Romantic Revival in its last stages. In the early poems and *The Waste Land* that rebellion is implicit. Eliot found a technique which, with the barest economy in the use of language, was nevertheless a verbal equivalent to his experience of personal challenge to the immediate past, to his sense of exile in the present, to the emotional and intellectual flavour of his apprehension of life on all sides of his nature.

Eliot's poetry is very difficult, and it seems inevitable that the poetry of the future will be difficult for the present generation of readers. It is Eliot who has made readers aware of where one great difficulty lies. We have become so used to only certain of our mental processes —the logical ones—rising to the level of expression in language, that the task of adjusting and accommodating the attention to respond in a new way to new material is a very hard one. And beyond that, modern poetry becomes increasingly difficult to read because not only have we to adjust our responses to the reception of very much more complex mental and emotional experiences, but we live in an age when new knowledge has altered the whole conception of the universe, just as it did at the Renaissance. The cosmos of the Renaissance is now as dead as the cosmos of the Dark Ages. A flood of new knowledge about the nature and behaviour of man and the universe he inhabits is being revealed, and the cry goes up that all human values are being undermined. It is only sentimental fictions, however, that are hurt by new knowledge. A knowledge of how the human mind really works, for instance, cannot alter the satisfaction of human emotional relationships, any more than a knowledge of the chemical components of the food we eat alters our appetite. But the vast influx of new intellectual concepts does have a very important bearing on poetry, for unless poetry is to die, which is unthinkable, the poet of the future must be able to attain to the same sort of solidity in his relation to Space and Time which we feel in Donne or Milton or Wordsworth. And it is impossible for the poet of today to do that, because, although the old cosmos is, scientifically speaking, dead, it is still alive to the majority of the livers of life in the present. Intellectually we may know that the old conceptions are no longer valid, but sub-consciously we still live in them: they are rooted too deeply into our hearts and minds and senses—above all they are rooted too deeply into our vocabulary—for us to change them. And this is the great difficulty for the poet. Poetry is words, and how is the poet to find language and rhythms which shall project the actual flavour of his experience in the universe of today? On the one hand the scientific vocabulary of his intellectual knowledge has no emotional associations and can therefore carry no emotional values, while on the other, the familiar language of the past, all the vocabulary of the old cosmogony which is loaded with sensuous and emotional suggestion and reverberation, will inevitably falsify his intellectual vision. When he struggles to bring the whole of himself into a genuine relationship with his experience, he cannot find a technique which shall 'organize' its reality; it is incoherent, dismembered and discrete; it is 'fused in no emotive furnace'. Hence the self-conscious roughness and harshness and distress of the rhythms of the sincere modern intellectual poet, and hence his own feeling of despair, and the feeling of despair of his reader. Hence, too, the croaking of those who cannot free themselves, even intellectually, from the old tradition, and lament dismally that the continuity of poetry is broken.

It is not broken, of that we may be sure. Let us remind ourselves again that new knowledge about man only widens, and does not alter, his consciousness. For thousands of years there have been men and women who have seen and felt experience in the form of poetry: for thousands of years there have been men and women who have been vitalized and soothed and enraptured by the communication of that poetry. What is our little pinpoint of an age that it should interrupt and block that mighty flow? Even in another generation much of the new knowledge may have been assimilated into the general race consciousness. A new language of image and symbol may have evolved, to which the eternal emotional responses of humanity will react: a new synthesis may have been achieved in which the new intellectual values are incorporated, while the old emotional ones remain untouched. Man may have become conscious that his whole nature has been revealed to him in a new way, that a new 'style' of life has sprung into being. And the creator of that new language of image and symbol which will bring that revelation of the new synthesis in the eternal elements of human experience, will be the great poet of the future.

APPENDICES

Prosody

I⊤ is clear from what has been said in the body of this book, that poetry is not a matter of laws of versification, or of any system of rules. The poet uses existing traditions or makes new forms for himself, just as it pleases him, and the merit of his verse depends on the living rhythms he creates and on nothing else. But the student of poetry should know the technical terms used in literary criticism, and the names of the various traditional forms of metrical arrangement. They are therefore summarized here.

The rhythmical unit in English poetry is commonly called a *foot*, and we have borrowed the classical names for describing the number and order and character of the syllables which form 'feet'. These may be either dissyllabic (formed of two syllables), or trisyllabic (formed of three syllables), and they are named as follows. A foot composed of a short syllable followed by a long is an *iamb*. A regular iambic line is,

The cŭr|fĕw tōlls | thĕ knēll | ŏf pārt|ĭng dāy.

A long syllable followed by a short is a *trochee*. The first foot in the following line is trochaic:

Lōvĕd Ĭ | nŏt hŏn|ŏur mōre.

A foot of two long syllables is a *spondee,* as in the last two feet here:

The cŭmb|rŏus ēl|ĕmēnts | —Ēarth, Flōod, | Āir, Fīre,

A long syllable followed by two short is a *dactyl:*

Tāke hĕr ŭp | tēndĕrlў.

And two short syllables followed by a long is an *anapaest:*

Ĭ ăm mōn|ărch ŏf āll | Ĭ sūrvēy.

Iambic and anapaestic feet (unstressed followed by stressed syllables) are known as 'rising rhythm', and trochaic and dactylic feet (stressed followed by unstressed syllables) are known as 'falling rhythm'.

There may be any number of feet in a line, but a sustained poem is seldom written in lines of less than two beats;

> Throw away thy rod
>   Throw away thy wrath;
> O my God,
>   Take the gentle path.

or more than eight.

So she arose from her home in the hills, and down through the
   blossoms that danced with their shadows,
Out of the blue of the dreaming distance, down to the heart
   of her lover she came.

VERSE FORMS

IT would be waste of time to attempt to catalogue all the various forms of stanza used by English poets, and any real student of prosody must consult Saintsbury's *History of English Prosody.* The following is a list of the 'named varieties' of verse forms in English poetry.

BLANK VERSE. Although it is usual to mean un-rhymed iambic pentameters when we speak of 'blank verse', any unrhymed verse form may be included in the name. There are some very beautiful unrhymed lyrics in English. The most famous are Collins's *Ode to Evening*, Lamb's *The Old Familiar Faces*, Tennyson's *Tears, Idle Tears*, and Blake's *To Spring*.

COUPLETS. The two most popular forms of this are the octosyllabic (four beats) and the Heroic couplet (five beats). Each form is capable of innumerable personal modifications and colouring. The student should compare the use made of the former by Milton, by Marvell, by the author of *Hudibras*, and by Coleridge: and of the latter by Chaucer in *The Prologue*, by Pope, by Keats in *Lamia* and Morris in *The Earthly Paradise*.

TERCETS. Verses of three lines on a single rhyme. Tennyson's *The Eagle* is an example:

> He clasps the crag with hookèd hands;
> Close to the sun in lonely lands,
> Ring'd with the azure world he stands.

or the *Threnos* in Shakespeare's *The Phoenix and Turtle*, where the movement is trochaic:

> Beauty, truth and rarity,
> Grace in all simplicity,
> Here inclosed in cinders lie.

TERZA RIMA. A poem in terza rima is written in stanzas of three lines linked by the interlocking of their rhymes, which are arranged aba, bcb, cdc, ded and so on. Dante's *Divina Commedia* is written in this metre, but there are not many examples of it in English poetry. The finest is Shelley's *Ode to the West Wind*.

O wild West Wind, thou breath of Autumn's being,
  Thou from whose unseen presence the leaves dead
Are driven, like ghosts from an enchanter fleeing,

  Yellow, and black, and pale, and hectic red,
Pestilence-stricken multitudes! O thou
  Who chariotest to their dark wintry bed

The wingèd seeds, where they lie cold and low,
  Each like a corpse within its grave, until
Thine azure sister of the Spring shall blow

  Her clarion o'er the dreaming earth....

QUATRAINS. Any four-lined stanza. The lines may be of any length, and the rhyme arrangement either abcb, abab, abba, aabb or aaba. It is impossible to give illustrations which can cover the ground of the various possible types of four, five, six, seven and eight lined stanzas. Their variations are legion.

RIME ROYAL. This is a seven-lined stanza in iambic pentameters rhymed ababbcc. It is the metre of Chaucer's *Troilus and Criseyde*, of Shakespeare's *The Rape of Lucrece* and of Masefield's *Dauber*.

From the besieged Ardea all in post,
Borne by the trustless wings of false desire,
Lust-breathed Tarquin leaves the Roman host,
And to Collatium bears the lightless fire,
Which, in pale embers hid, lurks to aspire,
  And girdle with embracing flames the waist
  Of Collatine's fair love, Lucrece the chaste.

OTTAVA RIMA. This is the most famous of the eight-lined stanza forms, and was brought from Italy by Sir Thomas Wyatt. It also is formed of iambic pentameters, with the rhyme scheme ababcc. It was Byron's favorite metre.

The angels were all singing out of tune,
  And hoarse with having little else to do,
Excepting to wind up the sun and moon,
  Or curb a runaway young star or two,
Or wild colt of a comet, which too soon
  Broke out of bounds o'er the ethereal blue,
Splitting some planet with its playful tail,
As boats are sometimes by a wanton whale.

SPENSERIAN STANZA. So called because it was
invented by Spenser for *The Faery Queen*. It is composed
of eight lines in iambic pentameter, with a final Alex-
andrine (a line of six beats), and the rhymes are
ababbcbcc. It was very popular among the early nine-
teenth century poets and is the metre of Keats's *The
Eve of St. Agnes*, of Byron's *Childe Harold* and of
Shelley's *Adonais*.

The One remains, the many change and pass;
Heaven's light forever shines, Earth's shadows fly;
Life, like a dome of many-coloured glass,
Stains the white radiance of Eternity,
Until Death tramples it to fragments.—Die
If thou wouldst be with that which thou dost seek!
Follow where all is fled!—Rome's azure sky,
Flowers, ruins, statues, music, words, are weak,
  The glory they transfuse with fitting truth to speak.

SONNET. There are many variations within the four-
teen lines which compose a sonnet, but the main types
are two, called usually the Petrarchan and the Shake-
spearian. The former is divided into an octave and a
sestet, the latter into three quatrains and a final couplet.
Several illustrations of both types have already been
quoted in this book.

ODE. The ode is the most loosely used term in metrical
description, and covers a very wide variety of poetic
form. There are regular and irregular odes. Regular, or

Horatian odes are written in stanzaic form. The first to be written in English were Spenser's *Prothalamion* and *Epithalamion*. Milton's *On the Morning of Christ's Nativity* uses another stanza form, and Keats created a form of his own, a quatrain, followed by a sestet, which is the scheme of the odes *To a Nightingale, On a Grecian Urn* and *To Melancholy*. In the *Ode to Autumn,* Keats introduced an extra line, giving an exquisitely melodious effect.

Another regular form of ode is the Pindaric, of which Gray's *Progress of Poetry* is the best example. What Cowley introduced into England as Pindaric Odes are not true Pindarics at all. He was too ignorant of classical metres to realize that the strophe, antistrophe and epode were intricate and elaborate, but quite regular structures. 'His idea of an ode,' as Sir Edmund Gosse says, 'was of a lofty and tempestuous piece of indefinite poetry conducted without sail or oar in whatever direction the enthusiasm of the poet chose to take it.' As a result, the ode in English poetry has remained a lofty, but indefinite form, offering the greatest freedom in metrical arrangement and in rhyme schemes. Wordsworth's *Intimations of Immortality* is generally considered the finest of these irregular odes in English poetry, but Tennyson's *The Death of Wellington,* and the odes of Coventry Patmore are worth study.

FRENCH LYRICAL FORMS. During the fourteenth and fifteenth centuries, the courtly poets of Provence elaborated a number of highly stylized lyric verse forms, which were never naturalized in England. Towards the end of the nineteenth century, however, a fashion for these forms was promoted by a group of English poets, of whom the chief were Swinburne, Austin Dobson, Andrew Lang, W. E. Henley and Edmund Gosse. Students interested in the subject should consult

Austin Dobson's introduction to *Latter Day Lyrics*,
Andrew Lang's *Ballads and Lyrics of Old France*, and
Gleeson White's *Ballades and Rondeaux*.

THE TRIOLET. A poem of eight lines with two
rhymes, arranged abaaabab.

> Rose kissed me today;
> Will she kiss me tomorrow?
> Let it be as it may,
> Rose kissed me today.
> But the pleasure gives way
> To a savour of sorrow,—
> Rose kissed me today,—
> *Will* she kiss me tomorrow?

THE RONDEAU AND RONDEL. These are allied
forms, the first of thirteen, the second of fourteen lines,
on two, or sometimes four rhymes, of which the scheme
varies. The lines, too, may be octosyllabic or decasyllabic.

The Gods are dead? Perhaps they are; Who knows?
   Living at least in Lempriere undeleted,
The wise, the fair, the awful, the jocose,
   Are one and all, I like to think, retreated
In some still land of lilacs and the rose.
Once high they sat, and high o'er earthly shows
   With sacrificial dance and song were greeted.
Once . . . long ago: but now the story goes,
      The gods are dead.

It must be true. The world a world of prose,
   Full-crammed with facts, in science swathed and sheeted,
Nods in a stertorous after-dinner doze.
Plangent and sad, in every wind that blows
   Who will may hear the sorry words repeated—
      The gods are dead.

                                   (W. E. Henley)

THE VILLANELLE. A light poem of nineteen lines, based on two rhymes, and divided into three-lined stanzas with a final quatrain.

> A dainty thing's the Villanelle.
>   Sly, musical, a jewel in rhyme,
> It serves its purpose passing well.
>
> A double-clappered silver bell
>   That must be made to clink in chime,
> A dainty thing's the Villanelle;
>
> And if you wish to flute a spell,
>   Or ask a meeting 'neath the lime,
> It serves its purpose passing well.
>
> You must not ask of it the spell,
>   Of organs grandiose and sublime—
> A dainty thing's the Villanelle;
>
> And filled with sweetness, as a shell
>   Is filled with sound, and launched in time,
> It serves its purpose passing well.
>
>   Still fair to see and good to smell
>   As in the quaintness of its prime,
>   A dainty thing's the Villanelle,
>   It serves its purpose passing well.
>   (W. E. Henley)

THE SESTINA. A form so complicated and intricate that it is rather a word puzzle than a poetic form. Students are referred for examples to the books quoted above.

THE BALLADE. The most popular of the French forms. There are two recognized types: one of three eight-lined stanzas, followed by a four-lined envoy; the other of three ten-lined stanzas, with a five-lined envoy.

Each is on four rhymes. Octosyllabic lines are usual for the eight-lined stanza, and decasyllabic for the ten-lined. The envoy was originally addressed to the Prince in whose service the court poet was writing. Perhaps the most famous ballade is Swinburne's *A Ballade of Fran-çois Villon, Prince of all Ballad-Makers*.

Bird of the bitter bright gray golden morn
    Scarce risen upon the dusk of dolorous years,
First of us all and sweetest singer born
    Whose far, shrill note the world of new men hears.
    Cleave the cold shuddering shade as twilight clears;
When song new-born put off the old world's attire
And felt its tune on her changed lips expire,
    Writ foremost on the roll of them that came
Fresh girt for service of the latter lyre,
    Villon, our sad bad glad mad brother's name!

Alas the joy, the sorrow, and the scorn,
    That clothed thy life with hopes and sins and fears,
And gave thee stones for bread and tares for corn
    And plume-plucked gaol-birds for thy starveling peers
    Till death clipt close their flight with shameful shears
Till shifts came short and loves were hard to hire,
When lilt of song nor twitch of twangling wire
    Could buy thee bread or kisses; when light fame
Spurned like a ball and haled through brake and briar,
    Villon, our sad bad glad mad brother's name!

Poor splendid wings so frayed and soiled and torn!
    Poor kind wild eyes so dashed with light quick tears!
Poor perfect voice, most blithe when most forlorn,
    That rings athwart the sea whence no man steers
    Like joy-bells crossed with death-bells in our ears!
What far delight has cooled the fierce desire
That like some ravenous bird was strong to tire
    On that frail flesh and soul consumed with flame,
But left more sweet than roses to respire,
    Villon, our sad bad glad mad brother's name?

ENVOI

Prince of sweet songs made out of tears and fire,
A harlot was thy nurse, a God thy sire;
   Shame soiled thy song, and song assoiled thy shame.
But from thy feet now death has washed the mire,
Love reads out first at head of all our quire,
   Villon, our sad bad glad mad brother's name.

Bibliography

TEXTS OF THE PRINCIPAL ENGLISH AND AMERICAN POETS

THIS is a reader's, not a student's, list. It includes collected editions only, and, wherever possible, standard texts in one volume have been chosen.

Arnold, Matthew. Poems, 1840-1867; with an introduction by Sir A. T. Quiller-Couch. Oxford edition, 1909.

Blake, William. Poems; edited and arranged, with a preface by John Sampson. 1921.

Bridges, Robert. Poetical works, excluding the eight dramas. Oxford edition, 1912.

————. Shorter Poems. Enlarged edition. Oxford, 1931.

Browning, Robert. Poetical works. Two volumes. John Murray, 1919.

Burns, Robert. Poetical works; edited by J. L. Robertson. Oxford edition, 1904.

Byron, George Gordon Noel, Lord. Complete poetical works; with introductory memoir by Sir Leslie Stephen. Globe edition. Macmillan, 1907.

Chaucer, Geoffrey. Complete works; edited by W. W. Skeat. Oxford edition, 1912.

Coleridge, Samuel Taylor. Poems; edited by E. H. Coleridge. 1912.

Cowper, William. Poetical works; edited by H. S. Milford. Oxford edition, 1926.

Crabbe, George. Poetical works; edited by A. J. and R. M. Carlyle. Oxford edition, 1908.

Crashaw, Richard. Poems; edited by L. C. Martin. Oxford, 1927.

Dickinson, Emily. Poems; edited by Thomas H. Johnson. Three volumes. Harvard, 1955. Poems. One volume. Little, 1960.

Donne, John. Poems; edited by H. J. C. Grierson. Oxford edition, 1929.

Dryden, John. Poems; edited with an introduction and notes by J. Serjeant. Oxford edition, 1910.

Emerson, Ralph Waldo. Poems. Centenary edition. 1904.

Hardy, Thomas. Collected poems. Macmillan, 1920.

Herbert, George. Poems; with an introduction by A. Waugh. Oxford edition, 1907.

Herrick, Robert. Poetical works; edited by F. W. Moorman. Oxford edition, 1921.

Hopkins, Gerard Manley. Poems; edited with notes by Robert Bridges. Second edition, with additional poems, and a critical introduction by Charles Williams. Oxford, 1930.

Keats, John. Poems; edited by E. de Selincourt. 1926.

Longfellow, Henry Wadsworth. Complete poetical works. Cambridge edition, 1908.

Lowell, James Russell. Poetical works. Cambridge edition, 1896.

Marvell, Andrew. Miscellaneous poems. Nonesuch Press. London, 1923.

————. Poems and Letters; edited by H. M. Margoliouth. Two volumes. 1927.

Meredith, George. Poetical works; with some notes by G. M. Trevelyan. 1912.

Meynell, Alice. Poems. 1923.

Milton, John. Poetical works; edited by H. C. Beeching. Oxford edition, 1904.

Morris, William. Prose and Poetry 1856-1870. Oxford edition, 1913.

Pope, Alexander. Poetical Works; edited by A. W. Ward. Globe edition, 1869.

Rossetti, Christina. Poetical works. Macmillan, 1904.

Rossetti, Dante Gabriel. Poems and Translations; with an introduction by John Buchan. London, 1924.

Shakespeare, William. Complete Works; edited by W. J. Craig. Oxford edition, 1913.

Shelley, Percy Bysshe. Poems; edited by Thomas Hutchinson. Oxford edition, 1919.

Spenser, Edmund. Poetical works; edited by J. C. Smith and E. de Selincourt. Oxford edition, 1912.

Swinburne, Algernon Charles. Poetical works. Two volumes. London, 1924.

Tennyson, Alfred, Lord. Works; edited by Hallam, Lord Tennyson. Globe edition, 1896.

Thompson, Francis. Poems; edited by the Rev. Terence L. Connolly. 1932.

Whitman, Walt. Poems; selected and edited by William Michael Rossetti. 1886.

————. Leaves of Grass; abridged edition with an introduction by Emory Holloway. 1926.

ANTHOLOGIES

American Poetry; from the beginning to Whitman. Edited by Louis Untermeyer. 1932.

An Anthology of English Verse; edited by John Drinkwater. 1924.

Come Hither; a collection of rhymes for all ages. Edited by Walter de la Mare. 1923.

The Golden Treasury of the best songs and lyrical poems in the English language; selected and arranged by Francis Turner Palgrave. With additional poems by contemporary writers. 1928.

Metaphysical lyrics and poems of the seventeenth century; edited by H. J. C. Grierson. 1921.

Modern American Poetry; edited by Louis Untermeyer. Fourth edition, 1930.

Modern British Poetry; edited by Louis Untermeyer. Third edition, 1930.

New Signatures. Poems by several hands. 1932.

The Oxford Book of English Verse; chosen by Sir Arthur Quiller-Couch. 1907.

The Oxford Book of Sixteenth Century Verse; chosen by E. K. Chambers. 1932.

The Oxford Book of Eighteenth Century Verse; chosen by D. Nichol Smith. 1926.

The Oxford Book of Regency Verse, 1798-1837; chosen by H. S. Milford. 1928.

The Oxford Book of Victorian Verse; chosen by Sir Arthur Quiller-Couch. 1925.

The Oxford Book of Ballads; chosen by Sir Arthur Quiller-Couch. 1910.

The Oxford Book of English Mystical Verse; chosen by D. H. S. Nicholson and A. H. E. Lee. 1916.

Poetry of the Nineties; edited by Clarence E. Andrews. 1926.

The School of Poetry. An anthology chosen for young readers. Edited by Alice Meynell. 1924.

Twentieth Century Poetry; edited by John Drinkwater, Henry Seidel Canby and William Rose Benet. 1930.

Twentieth Century Poetry; an anthology, edited by Harold Monro. 1929.

CRITICISM

THIS list of critical books on poetry is not a long one, but perhaps for that reason it may be more valuable to the reader than a mere catalogue of titles based on no principle of careful choice. The aim in compiling it has been to mention only such books as possess living values for the reader of poetry. These values are of various kinds, and the books are not necessarily recommended because the author of this book agrees with the opinions expressed in them. Some of them are sound, honest, penetrating, scholarly criticism on conventional and traditional lines: some boldly challenge all accepted convention and tradition: some pursue original lines of thought: some treat their themes in an unusual and provocative way. More space has been allotted to the criticism of today than to that of yesterday, since there are already many bibliographies which deal generously with the books published ten to twenty years back. A few notes have been added, as indications of the character and contents of some of the lesser known volumes.

THE THEORY OF POETRY

Abercrombie, Lascelles. The Theory of Poetry. 1924.
———. The Idea of Great Poetry. 1925.
Arnold, Matthew. Culture and Anarchy. 1869.
———. Essays in Criticism. 1868.
———. Essays in Criticism, second series. 1888.
———. On Translating Homer. 1861.
Bradley, A. C. Oxford Lectures on Poetry. 1914.
    Excellent essays on *Poetry for Poetry's sake, Shelley's View of Poetry,* and *The Letters of Keats.*
Brémond, Henri. Prayer and Poetry; a contribution to poetical theory. 1927.
———. La Poesie pure. Paris. 1926.
Coleridge, Samuel Taylor. Biographia Literaria; edited by J. Shawcross. Two volumes. 1927.
Drinkwater, John. The Lyric. 1916.
    A short, but very stimulating little book.
Eastman, Max. The Enjoyment of Poetry. 1914.
———. The Literary Mind. 1931.
    The last book combines a strong plea for the recognition of psychology as the essential basis for criticism, with a slashing attack on traditional methods.

Eliot, Thomas Stearns. The Sacred Wood: essays on poetry and criticism. 1920.

———. Homage to John Dryden. 1924.

———. For Lancelot Andrewes: essays on style and order. 1928.

Empson, William. Seven Types of Ambiguity. London, 1930. At times over-ingenious and repetitive, but a most valuable and original analysis of the apprehension of poetry.

Graves, Robert. On English Poetry: being an irregular approach to the psychology of the art, from evidence mainly subjective. 1922.

———. Poetic Unreason and other studies. 1925.

Graves, Robert, and Riding, Laura. A Survey of Modernist Poetry. 1927.
A provocative, but not very convincing championship.

Jameson, R. D. Poetry and Plain Sense (a note on the poetic method of T. S. Eliot). 1931. National Tsing Hua University publications. Peiping.

Keats, John. Letters.

Ker, William Paton. The Art of Poetry. 1923.

Leavis, F. R. New Bearings in English Poetry. London. 1932. Impolite criticism of the nineteenth and early twentieth century, and some very interesting essays on T. S. Eliot, Ezra Pound and Gerard Manley Hopkins.

Lowes, John Livingston. The Road to Xanadu; a study in the way of the imagination. 1927.

———.Convention and revolt in poetry. Second edition. 1930.

Lucas, F. L. Eight Victorian Poets. 1930.

Murry, John Middleton. Aspects of Literature. 1920.

———. Countries of the Mind. 1922.

———. Countries of the Mind. Second series. 1931.

———. The Problem of Style. 1922.
At his best Middleton Murry is one of the most penetrating and revealing of critics.

Pater, Walter. Appreciations. 1889.
Contains the famous essay on *Style*.

Patmore, Coventry. Religio Poetae. 1893.

———. Principle in Art. 1896.

Read, Herbert. Reason and Romanticism. 1926.

———. Form in Modern Poetry. 1932.
This is an interesting study in the approach to the problem of poetic form from a psychological basis.

Richards, Ivor Armstrong. Principles of Literary Criticism. 1924.

————. Science and Poetry. 1926.

————. Practical Criticism. 1929.

Sewell, Arthur. The Physiology of Beauty. Kegan Paul, London. 1931.
   Full of very interesting material on the relation of philosophy and psychology to the experiences of art in general and poetry in particular.

Shelley, Percy Bysshe. Literary and Philosophical Criticism; edited with an introduction by J. Shawcross. 1909.

Wordsworth, William. Literary Criticism; edited with an introduction by Nowell C. Smith. 1905.

Williams, Charles. Poetry at Present. 1930.

————. The English Poetic Mind. 1932.

Wilson, Edmund. Axel's Castle.
   Excellent essays on the "Modernist" writers.

Yeats, W. B. Essays. 1924.
   This contains a particularly interesting essay on *The Symbolism of Poetry*.

THE PRACTICE OF POETRY
PROSODY AND TECHNIQUE

Andrews, Clarence E. The writing and reading of verse. 1918.
   Contains an immense amount of valuable information.

Barfield, Owen. Poetic Diction; a study in meaning. 1928.

Ker, William Paton. Form and Style in Poetry. 1928.
   Full of sound scholarship and pregnant ideas.

Omond, T. S. English Metrists: being a sketch of English prosodical criticism from Elizabethan times to the present day. 1921.

Rylands, George H. W. Words and Poetry. 1928.
   Full of stimulating ideas and illustrations, and written with lively enthusiasm.

Saintsbury, George. A History of English Prosody. Three volumes. 1923.

Snyder, Edward D. Hypnotic Poetry: a study of trance-inducing technique in certain poems and its literary significance; with a foreword by J. H. Leuba. 1930.

Untermeyer, Louis. The Forms of Poetry: a pocket dictionary of verse. 1926.
   A tabulation of the technical terms of poetry.

References

Index